Student Self-Discipline
in the Classroom
& Beyond

Patricia M. McCormack, Ed. D.

Faithful Past – Faith-filled Future

100

1904-2004

NCEA

NATIONAL CATHOLIC EDUCATIONAL ASSOCIATION

Published in the United States of America by the National Catholic Educational Association.

ISBN No.   1-55833-316-9
Part No.   ADM-22-1304

Table of Contents

Self-Discipline:
A Gospel-Driven Term

QUICK-WITTED KYLA withholds a clever retort to Lisa's taunting. What prudence! Jillian reports to her service project moderator even though she does not feel like it. Her determination feels like long-suffering some days! Though Eric deeply desires to become school president he refuses to participate in the smear campaign tactics of his opponents. Some friends are amazed by his integrity. Stephanie refrains from alcohol at a party hosted by the " in crowd." Her fortitude may eliminate her from future activities with some peers. Having completed his assignments, Benjamin began his homework while waiting for the teacher to return to the class. He acted responsibly and, upon return, the teacher complimented him for using good judgment. Although the director and several other programmers left at noon, Carol remained on task until closing time. Some folks might say that she is conscientious or just plain "nuts." Carol calls it honesty! Mark's parent responds kindly and calmly to a barrage of questions from his four-year-old brother. Mark asked, *"Where can I find patience like yours? I'd like to buy some!"* These folks have a common thread that weaves their scenarios into the fabric of character. What is it? What is core to the practice of virtues like prudence, determination, integrity, fortitude, responsibility, honesty, or patience? I suggest that it is self-discipline. Kyla, Jillian, Eric, Stephanie, Benjamin, Carol, and Mark's parent know and live the meaning of discipleship.

Discipline is the ability to listen to the voice of another, to understand the message, and to act upon it appropriately in freedom, without external impetus. The word discipline, derived from the Latin *disciplina*, means to grasp or to take instruction.[1] Far from needing outside coercion or extrinsic motivation, a disciple is self-motivated to make the message of another his/her own and to translate that word into action. The disciple wants to become like the master, to freely follow in the footsteps of the master, to think like the master, to speak like the master, to respond like the master, to hold the values of the master, and to be known publicly as a disciple of the master. Simultaneously, discipleship becomes the goal, the privilege, and the reward of the faithful follower. When the Master is Jesus Christ, the slogan, *"What would Jesus do?"* is the supreme value for the disciple.

The Primary Purpose of Catholic Education

The Catholic School is a privileged place to cultivate discipleship through attitudes, approaches, and policies that reflect the principles of Catholic identity. The culture of discipleship must punctuate the rhythm of the school day and permeate its classrooms, athletic fields, laboratories, playgrounds, and life choices away from school. Leading souls to a vital relationship with Christ is the primary purpose of Catholic education. Helping students to recognize the voice of Christ and to respond to his message is fundamental to the evangelizing mission of the Church. Our students live in a world of many voices, messages, distractions, and promises that deafen the ears of the soul. It is our task to assist them to develop *"ears open to obedience"* (Ps. 40:7). Obedience, like discipline, is positive and leads to life. And like discipline, the word originates in the Latin language *ob + audiere*. It means to listen, an active listening that leads to a positive action response. Discipleship requires ongoing discernment: recognizing the voice of God calling us to live the Christ-life in the particulars of daily encounters and choices. The author of Deuteronomy expressed the desire of God for us this way:

"For this command which I enjoin on you today . . . is something very near to you, already in your mouths and in your hearts; you have only to carry it out. Here, then, I have today set before you life and prosperity, death and doom. If you obey the commandments of the Lord, your God, which I enjoin on you today, loving him, and walking in his ways, and keeping his commandments, statutes and decrees, you will live . . . If, however, you turn away your hearts and will not listen, but are led astray and adore and serve other gods, I tell you now that you will certainly perish. . . I have set before you life and death, the blessing and the curse. Choose life, then, that you and your descendants may live, by loving the Lord, your God, heeding his voice, and holding fast to him. For that will mean life for you . . ." (Deut. 30:19-20).

This author urged his listeners to choose life, a theme Jesus repeated: *"I came that they might have life and have it to the full"* (Jn. 10:10).

Attitudes and behaviors that create, mend, heal, invite, forgive, include others, share, initiate, unite, build up, and contribute to improvement are life-giving choices. Life-giving choices free a person to be open, honest, peace-loving, and approachable. When Kyla held back words that would hurt and Jillian was faithful to her promise to give weekly service, when Eric "took the high road" of integrity, the results were life-giving for the students concerned, as well as the overflow of goodness to the community. Those students displayed self-discipline and self-mastery. They "heard" God's words of life. They understood their meaning and price. And they freely responded "yes" to life and to the author of life. Repeated choices for life lead to the development of self-discipline and self-control. A contemporary rendering of a wise saying reminds us that all habits begin with a single act and repeated acts shape character:

Plant a thought; reap an act.
Plant an act; reap a habit.
Plant a habit; reap a virtue or vice.
Plant a virtue or vice; reap a character.
Plant a character; reap a destiny. [2]

The aim of Catholic educators is to involve students in the practice of choosing life through efforts that are persistent and pervasive. Life-blocking choices, on the other hand, bring sorrow and destruction. They are attitudes and behaviors that separate, isolate, destroy, exclude, wound, deceive, divide, manipulate, tear down, and alienate. The fruits of life-blocking choices fill the daily news, leaving us fearful, broken in spirit, discouraged, distrustful, and disappointed. Had Stephanie ignored her inner voice and accepted alcohol at the party she would have opened herself to the possibility of lying to cover up her behavior, a breakdown in communication with her parents. Had Benjamin used the occasion of the teacher's prolonged absence from the room to fool around, any number of accidents could have occurred; at the least there would have been a rupture in his relationship with his teacher.

Students of all ages can grasp the concept of life-giving vs. life-blocking choices. If the concept is understood and internalized, students will be more likely to recognize the voice of God during daily encounters. At every age level a teacher can facilitate a class discussion, using examples of life-giving behaviors and their consequences. Through shared examples, stories, cartoons, or film, the class can give age-appropriate examples of such life-giving choices and behaviors. When children demonstrate life-giving behavior it might be sufficient to give a wink, an "A-OK" finger sign, a smile, or nod while pointing to the icon, poster, or illustration that represents such behaviors. The process can be repeated for life-blocking choices. One teacher made attractive vocabulary panels of the terms given by the students, i.e., sharing, including others, apologizing, or ignoring others, critical remarks, put-downs, and ridicule and used the space above the chalkboard in the front of the room to display the words and phrases. The command "*Choose Life*" served as the centerpiece. "Life-Giving" words were placed on the left and "Life-Blocking" on the right. This display served as a focal point throughout the year. It was sufficient for the teacher to point to the "Choose Life" centerpiece or to hold up one finger representing the "Life-Giving" side or two fingers that represented the "Life-Blocking" side. Students quickly assumed ownership of the "one finger, two fingers" sign language. The silent signal became a respectful, instructive aid that encouraged positive behavior and contributed to formation in self-discipline.

Children who understand the concept of life-giving and life-blocking choices and the natural consequences of such choices experience the first stages of wisdom. During a discussion of discipleship, McCormack has offered parents an illustration of this dynamic. This principle of cause and effect offers helpful information to teachers as well:

> "A child (student) who hears and understands the meaning of Jesus' law of love would be more likely to live the spirit of the Commandments and experience the positive results of disciplined choices. He would willingly respect God, God's name, and the things of God; participate in Sunday worship; lovingly fulfill the wishes of a parent or other adult in authority; respect and protect life in all ways; exercise control and reverence in sexual matters; develop wholesome relationships; be honest and responsible with material things as well as with the reputation of others; keep relational commitments and honor the personal relationships of others. A self-disciplined child knows and accepts personal boundaries; exercises freedom with responsibility; tries to cooperate; upholds the common good; and accepts the logical consequences of her choices. Self-discipline, self-esteem, and character formation are interrelated concepts. They share basic principles that are rooted in formation provided by parents."[3]

A Word about the Primary Educators of Children

The scope of this book is limited to consideration of the Catholic school as a catalyst of self-discipline and discipleship; it must be clearly established, however, that parents are the primary teachers of their children and that formation rests fundamentally with parents.[4]

The ability or inability of parents to provide that foundation has a great impact in the classroom and is a support or obstacle to the vocation of teachers to contribute to the holistic development of their students. Catholic school educators must be creative in responding to the needs of parents and help parents to respond adequately to the formation of their children. It has been the subject of numerous Church documents.[5] The Congregation for Catholic Education expressed succinctly the concern raised in other Church documents:

> *"The first and primary educators of children are their parents. The school is aware of this fact but, unfortunately, the same is not always true of the families themselves; it is the school's responsibility to give them this awareness."*[6]

McCormack conducted research with parents to determine how well Catholic elementary schools functioned as agents of parent formation, i.e., helping parents to feel knowledgeable and adequate to foster the formation of their children. The findings imply that a need exists to clarify the elements of identity formation and to communicate both information and strategies to parents. McCormack summarized:

> *"Despite the expressed need of parents for help in the parenting role; the emphasis of the Roman Church and the American Church on the importance of formative parenting; and the view of Post Vatican II literature that the role of the Catholic school includes the responsibility to provide formative parenting assistance, the researcher located scant literature related to the Catholic school as an agent of formative parenting assistance."*[7]

The issue of providing formative support for parents warrants vigorous pursuit, but since parenting is not the focus of this book, formation remarks have been addressed to the Catholic school and its teachers. Of course, the work of teachers is more easily accomplished when the foundation has been established in the family and parental support is evident throughout the school year. Even in cases where the home environment is more of an obstacle than a support, however, a teacher can be the catalyst that leads a student to discipleship.

The Expanded Role of the Catholic School in Formation

Today, however, even believing parents have a formidable task, given an increasingly "secular" culture. Therefore, as it has always done, the Catholic school works with parents to reinforce and extend the Christian formation of their children. The Sacred Congregation for Education has said that: *"The Catholic school has as its specific duty the complete Christian formation of its pupils, and this task is of special significance today because of the inadequacy of the family and society."*[8]

Since the publication of this document, Church literature as well as the addresses of John Paul II have repeated or expanded on the need for Catholic schools to continue to work with parents in the formation of their children. As McCormack reported:

> *"Church literature from the 1980's (John Paul II, 1981, 1988; Congregation for Catholic Education, 1982, 1988) underscored the need for the Catholic school to assume leadership in providing total personal formation to both parents and students. In the apostolic exhortation* **On the Family***, John Paul II (1981) called for 'the renewal of the Catholic school to give special attention both to the parents and to the pupils and to the formation of a perfect educating community' (#40). In the document* **Lay Catholics in Schools: Witnesses to Faith** *(1982), the Congregation for Catholic Education cited influences in society that were harmful or counterproductive to holistic formation and summarized that because 'the family, on its own, is less and less able to confront all of these serious problems, the presence of the [Catholic] school becomes more and more necessary' (#13). The document noted that the value and importance of the Catholic school were fundamental to holistic formation and it reaffirmed that 'the school entered into the specific mission of the Church' (#13). John Paul II (1988) hailed the Catholic school as an important place for formation and emphasized that the participation of parents in school life, besides being always necessary and without substitution, is no longer enough."*[9]

Supporting parent efforts to provide for the total formation of their children remains the constant goal of Catholic Schools. Now, as at the time of initial establishment, Catholic schools strive to provide skills beyond the competency of the home and to preserve and transmit the faith within a social climate that is sometimes hostile to Catholic teachings. Immersed in a secular culture that presents stumbling blocks and challenges to Gospel-living, "parents report that they experience confusion, inferiority, limitation and bewilderment in promoting the unique life formation needs of their children and they approach their vocation conscious of their limitations."[10]

Post-Vatican II literature concurs with parent-expressed concerns that influences in society are harmful or counterproductive to the holistic formation of children. Motivated by pastoral concern, post-Vatican II literature reveals a desire for the progressive expansion of the role of the Catholic School in the work of personal formation. As the educational arm of the Church, Catholic educators have seen their role evolve from: (1) helpmates to parents through support, partnership, and assistance, (2) to being regarded as experts in the transmission of Christian culture, i.e., a systematic presentation of Christian social ethics[11] and "moral criteria that will enable them [students] to remain objective and independent when faced with the prevailing attitudes and habits of society,"[12] (3) to assuming the lead in providing for the complete Christian formation of students through the integration of faith and life in a life-long process of conversion leading students to put on the mind of Christ, to share their lives with him, to overcome individualism and to "discover their specific vocation to live responsibly in a community with others."[13] The effectiveness of the Catholic school as an agent of total Christian formation is predicated upon four characteristics: "the Catholic school as a place of integral education of the human person through a clear educational project of which Christ is the foundation; its ecclesial and cultural identity; its mission of education as a work of love; its service to society; and the traits which should characterize the educating community."[14]

Moral leadership is never an easy task; it has been made more complex by the aspects of modern culture that were noted in *The Catholic School on the Threshold of the Third Millennium*. In this document the challenges facing Catholic schools today are noted:

"The school is undoubtedly a sensitive meeting point for the problems which besiege this restless end of the millennium. The Catholic school is thus confronted with children and young people who experience the difficulties of the present time: pupils who shun effort, are incapable of self-sacrifice and perseverance and who lack authentic models to guide them, often even in their own families. In an increasing number of instances they are not only indifferent and non-practicing, but also totally lacking in religious or moral formation. To this we must add— on the part of numerous pupils and families—a profound apathy where ethical and religious formation is concerned, to the extent that what is in fact required of the Catholic school is a certificate of studies or, at the most, quality instruction and training for employment. The atmosphere we have described produces a certain degree of pedagogical tiredness, which intensifies the ever increasing difficulty of conciliating the role of the teacher with that of the educator in today's context."[15]

The conditions cited by the Congregation are enough to overwhelm the best teachers. Teachers should not despair, however, because they trust Jesus who has called them to this mission. In the postlude to the Gospel of Matthew, Jesus commissions all who believe in him to go to all nations and baptize in the name of the Trinity, to teach them to carry out everything that he commanded, and to do so in the knowledge that Jesus would be with them always (Matt. 28.19-20). The task of Catholic school teachers is to help students learn how to hear this Word. That is discipline.[16]

Discipline Defined

Discipline in this context means hearing the voice of another, understanding the meaning of what is heard, and applying the message freely and appropriately to the situation. The voice is that of Jesus: expressed in scripture, discerned in prayer, or spoken through agents of formation, e.g., parents, teachers, responsible adults, events, or good friends. Hearing and responding to the voice of God engenders virtues like charity, joy, peace, patience, goodness, kindness, generosity, long-suffering, mildness, gentleness, faithfulness, fidelity, modesty, self-control, and self-restraint. These are the behaviors shown by Kyla, Jillian, Eric, Stephanie, Benjamin, Carol, and Mark's parent.

Discipline is fostered or cultivated through (1) attitude, (2) approach, (3) policy, (4) behavior, (5) teaching, and (6) conversation, formal or informal, that is respectful of the student and leads him or her to become inner-directed, responsible, responsive, and cooperative. When classroom discipline and teacher-to-student communication is an instructive, respectful, proactive, and positive process it contributes to the cultivation of discipleship and Christian character.

The Purpose of this Book

The focus of this book is to invite readers to consider discipline as a mindset; not simply as a program of behavior management. Discipline programs have been developed by others.[17] It is not the purpose of this book to critique existing programs for school discipline. Rather, the purpose of this book is five-fold:

- to define the word discipline within a positive, gospel-driven context;
- to transform notions of discipline from the negative (e.g., control, coercion, punishment, and retaliation) to the positive (e.g., inner-direction, responsibility, cooperation, and responsiveness);
- to consider the way the grace of vocation , i.e., the divine mission of evangelization versus job security, influences the attitudes, approaches, and policies that teachers use to foster growth in self-discipline;
- to delineate teacher skills that are foundational to effective practices of discipline;
- and, to share the wisdom of teachers from various schools in the United States and Canada who motivate students to become active agents of self-discipline through positive, pro-active attitudes, and structures.

It is hoped that readers will review their own philosophies and approaches to students in light of the themes presented in this book. It is also hoped that readers will find validation of their own disciplinary practices as well as a storehouse of new strategies and proactive procedures for classroom management that lead students to form decision-making skills and growth in self-discipline in an atmosphere of joy and freedom. A final hope is that readers will consider discipline and discipleship as aspects that motivate personal reflection, which reclaims the grace of vocation, and renewed commitment to serving Christ as a catalyst in the formation of students. "That Christ may reign" is the inspiration of this book, the purpose of Catholic schools, and the animating principle of all educators who accept their profession as a vocation.

CHAPTER ONE

To Create a Culture of Discipleship

CATHOLIC SCHOOL EDUCATORS can cultivate a culture of discipleship through principles that permeate the environment of the school. These principles are rooted in the belief that all children are created in the image and likeness of God. Thus each person is an expression of God and, as such, is of infinite potential. Catholic schools and school personnel must validate this reality in attitude, approach, and policy, and must express it with consistency. Reverence for the dignity of each person and the desire to help each one reach this God-given potential is the fundamental principle in Catholic education. The Catholic educator who is respectful to students during formal and informal teaching and through conversations, planned or impromptu, contributes to a culture of discipleship that embodies this belief. Respect begets respect and leads students to become discerning, internally motivated, responsive, and responsible. School policy, pro-active classroom practices, and student correction that is instructive and respectful fosters growth in self-discipline.

A positive approach to the concept of self-discipline must be a cornerstone of school life if a sense of discipline, i.e., personal responsibility, is to take root in students. As Thomas Lickona reminds us, *"discipline must help students develop moral reasoning self discipline, and respect for others. The emphasis should not be on extrinsic rewards and punishment, but on following rules because it's the right thing to do—because it respects the rights and needs of others. When students break a rule, consequences should include moral dialogue that makes explicit reference to the relevant virtues.*"[18] All school events, whether school assemblies, gatherings around the flag, participation in the liturgy, enrichment presentations or class field trips, provide opportunities for formation in discipline. They also are opportunities to raise awareness of the common good, social graces, and responsibility to others, i.e., to concepts and events larger than oneself. An environment conducive to the development of self-discipline is encouraged through teacher practices that are informal, ordinary, and routine, such as, e.g.,

- transition activities between subjects or classes;
- focus assignments at the beginning of class;
- soft music;
- routine procedures for the beginning and ending of the school day;
- a published code of behavior along with discussions that illustrate cause, effect, predictable consequences, and procedures for self-correction;
- and, routines for correcting work, submitting assignments, or distributing materials.

The approach to self-discipline is crucial. When it is positive, students are more likely to become inner-directed, responsible, cooperative, and responsive; when negative, i.e., characterized by control, coercion, unexplained demands, punishment, retaliation, or cold detachment, students are likely to become angry, resentful, defensive, defiant, or belligerent.

Through school policies, procedures, and in their persons, teachers should express attitudes of discipline that are expressive of gospel mandates. As the Catholic bishops of the United States have said: "*In the Catholic school's educational project there is no separation between the time for learning and time of for formation, between acquiring notions and growing in wisdom.*"[19] When Gospel attitudes are an intrinsic part of the educational environment, students are enabled to recognize, accept, and embrace the notion that they are created in the image and likeness of God, and to give expression to that reality in their daily lives.

Discipline: What It Is and What It Is Not

Discipline is not about managing behavior, policing, controlling, or punishment; rather, it is aimed at helping students to develop the ability to listen to another's voice, to understand the message, and to act upon it appropriately with autonomy. Discipline, therefore, is not reactive, but initiatory and community-minded. Discipline does not seek retaliation. It seeks growth, wholeness, peace, and personal development. Consequently, the disciplinarian is creative in responding (not reacting) when the need for intervention arises so as to turn a poor choice, mistake, or sin into an experience of growth. Rather than focusing on the individual at the expense of his or her social rights, i.e., *"I have a right to my opinion," "It was my turn to erase the chalkboard," "I don't like him,"* or *"I want to use the computer,"* the disciplinarian focuses on the action and the effect that the action has on the community. Gospel discipline focuses on avoidance of sin rather than on self-interest, explicit in attitudes, such as: *"what's in it for me?"* or *"how far can I go?"* or *"how much can I get away with?"* Positive attitudes of discipline foster intrinsic motivation, self-control and the attitude of right-for-the-sake-of-right. Discipline is not about bartering rewards and punishments. It is about asking the question, *"What am I called to do? What am I inspired to be?"* and *"Who calls me to make life-giving choices?"*

My approach has been informed by the research and presentations of William J. Hudson, Associate Executive Director in the Department of Secondary Schools at the National Catholic Educational Association (NCEA). He has organized his reflections on school discipline by asserting the biblical basis of authority and discipline and the necessity of a process of moral reasoning, as well as the naming both positive goals and negative beliefs. His insights, along with those of Thomas Lickona and Alfred Kohn, have influenced the following discussion;[20] these ideas are summarized in **Table 1**.

TABLE 1
DEFINING DISCIPLINE

Discipline is about . . .	Discipline is not about . . .
learning to recognize the life-giving voice of God in persons and events; understanding the message; and acting upon it appropriately with autonomy in freedom	managing the behavior of a student;policing or controlling
developing expectations, norms and structures that: • inspire life-giving moral thinking • deal compassionately with hurtful behavior choices • make hurt less likely to happen in the first place	Unconnected, isolated rules or hoops to jump through, which breed resentment and revenge
fostering community – a place where students experience both individual nourishment and mutual caring; a place where relationship is fostered	Safeguarding a collective – a place where children are exhorted to silence their own needs for the sake of conformity; overcoming private preference in order to serve the group
active decision making	passive conformity
cooperative relationships – learning to see things as others see them; to seek a broader view outside oneself	self-centeredness
recognizing, accepting, embracing each child as "imago Dei" – an image of God who is a unique gift of God	Competition
being pro-active, instructive, respectful, and positive	being re-active, overbearing, demanding, bullying, or negative
becoming inner-directed, responsible, responsive, cooperative	becoming extrinsically motivated by rewards and punishments
Freedom	Coercion

seeking growth, wholeness, peace, and personal development	seeking control, retaliation, and pay-back
focusing on the action and its affect on the community	focusing on the individual at the expense of social rights and self-esteem
focusing on how to grow out of sin; asking "What am I called to be?" or "What am I inspired to be?"	fostering self-interest; a "What's in it for me?" attitude; "How far can I go?" or "How much can I get away with?"
rights and wrongs that teach lessons	do's and don'ts of managing behavior
"working with" a student	"doing to" a student
cultivating an attitude of: "How can I help?" "What can I do *for* you?"	cultivating an attitude of: "What consequence should you suffer?" "What can I do *to* you?"

Correction that Leads to Conversion

The goal of Christian discipleship is conversion, not compliance; a change of heart, not the mere performance of teacher expectation. As Hudson has articulated it, *"The tension is between getting kids to do what the adult wants them to do and building an environment within which the child chooses to do the right thing...[Alfred] Kohn goes further in saying that compliance is doing to students as opposed to doing things with students."*[21] This is another way of defining the difference between extrinsic and intrinsic motivation. As Hudson says: *"Intrinsic motivation is for a child to refrain from talking back to a teacher because that student knows and understands that it is wrong. Extrinsic motivation is the same student refraining from talking back, but in the case he does so because he/she fears the consequence, such as detention or a trip to the principal's office. Intrinsic motivation is internal to the student and displays to commitment to social responsibility. Extrinsic motivation is external or outside the individual and is simply conformity or compliance."*[22]

The importance of conversion and its distinction from compliance has been articulated, not only by those directly concerned with the education of the young, but also by Catholic systematic theologians. One, Bernard F. Lonergan, explains conversion as basic to Christian living:

> *"By conversion is understood a transformation of the subject* [student] *and his world. . . . a resultant change of course and direction . . . Conversion, as lived, affects conscious and intentional operations . . . directs his gaze, pervades his imagination . . . enriches his understanding, guides his judgments, reinforces his decisions."*[23]

Lonergan distinguishes among intellectual, moral, and religious conversion. Though all are interconnected and all lead to discipleship, the focus of this book is moral conversion which ". . . *changes the criterion of one's decisions and choices from satisfactions to values. . . . Moral conversion consists in opting for the truly good, even for value against satisfaction when value and satisfaction conflict."* Interaction and dialogue in instances of correction can be vehicles for moral conversion that move us from needing to be ". . . *persuaded, cajoled, ordered or compelled to do what is right"* to *"the existential moment when we discover for ourselves that our choosing affects ourselves . . . and that it is up to each of us to decide for himself what he is to make of himself."*[24] Hudson notes that the word for conversion in the New Testament is *metanoia*, i.e., a radical internal process of changing the person, both inside and out, one that is lifelong.[25]

Catholic educators should be instruments of such grace for students. Correction, in the view of B. Coloroso, *"is a process that gives life to learning; it is restorative, and it invites reconciliation. Its goal is to instruct, to teach, to guide and to help children develop self-discipline – an ordering of the self from the inside, not an imposition from the outside. In giving life to our children's learning, we are concerned not with mere compliance but with inviting our children to delve deep into themselves and reach beyond what is required or expected."*[26] Thus conversion is quite different from compliance. The contrast between them is provided in **Table 2**.

TABLE 2
CONTRAST: CONVERSION VERSUS COMPLIANCE

ISSUE	CONVERSION	COMPLIANCE
Definition	Internal process of thinking and willing signified by a radical turning around: a change of heart, an opening of mind, returning home to the soul	External response to act in accordance with requirements, regulations, expectations
Goal	Learning	Conforming
Focus	Underlying motives and values Choosing to know the good, desire the good, and do the good	On behavior Doing what the teacher wants
Climate	Safety, warmth, trust, nurturing, supportive	Threatening, cold, fearful, void of relationship
Mindset	What do students require in order to flourish? What can I do to provide those things?	How do I make students do what I want them to do?
Motivation	Intrinsic motivation Internal compass Commitment to social responsibility Create a sense of personal power (autonomy)	Extrinsic motivationFear of consequences External conformity Powered by another; rely on another for decision-making
Approach	Teacher considers misbehavior as a "teachable moment" Employs moral dialogue Links choices with community values Challenges with high expectations Fosters contrition	Teacher seeks to control and dominate Punition-driven Fosters resentment and defiance
Suspension Or Expulsion	Child is removed to create personal growth opportunity and to protect the common good. Hope for reconciliation and eventual return	Child is removed for control, rather than rehabilitation

As Table 2 shows, compliance is driven by what the adult wants, whereas conversion places the onus on the child, who must choose to do the right thing precisely because it is the life-giving choice. Conversion is internally-motivated, not externally controlled. The teacher caught up in compliance is concerned only about making students do something, whereas the teacher who makes conscious effort to be a catalyst of conversion wants students to ask themselves what is the right thing to do and provides a venue for that opportunity. Its essence is communal and this is the heart of the formative endeavor. Kohn has defined community as:

> "[Community] is a place in which students feel cared about and are encouraged to care about each other. They experience a sense of being valued and respected; the children matter to one another and to the teacher. They have come to think in the plural: they feel connected to each other; they are part of an "us." And as a result of all this, they feel safe in their classes, not only physically but emotionally."[27]

Conversion enables the person to embrace commitment to social responsibility and creates a sense of personal power. Autonomy lies within; therefore, the converted student does not need authority figures present in order to make life-giving decisions. Consider the worth of autonomy in an instance like drug use. Though schools have responded to the national crisis with anti-drug programs, the only truly effective response is personal autonomy and personal self-discipline.

The crucial question, therefore, is how to move students from correction to conversion, rather than simply to compliance. As Hudson has noted, a gospel-driven approach takes note of the way Jesus viewed the situation. He regarded the sinner as a person made in the image of God and treated each person with respect. He spoke the truth in love, that is, his words were chosen to call forth reflection, conversion and life-to-the-full; they were not motivated by a desire to hurt or demean another. It was not his intention to sting, although truth does sting when a person is living in opposition to it, as in the case of the moneychangers in the temple or the men who were stoning the adulterous woman. He avoided defending himself (Mt. 27: 12-14). He placed before his listeners teaching that stirred the soul (Mk. 12: 28-34). He asked clarifying questions (Mk. 9:33-35). He honored the exercise of free will (Jn. 6: 66-69). He permitted people to experience the consequence of their choices (Mk. 10: 17-22). He forgave without holding a grudge (Jn. 20: 19). He called the sinner to new life (Jn. 8: 10). He offered new beginnings (Lk. 19: 1-10). Catholic educators are called to follow in his steps. We are called to forgive as the Lord forgives. We are challenged to create a climate for conversion. As St. Paul wrote:

> "Because you are God's chosen ones, holy and beloved, clothe yourselves with heartfelt mercy, with kindness, humility, meekness, and patience. Bear with one another; forgive whatever grievances you have against one another. Forgive as the Lord has forgiven you. Over all these virtues put on love, which binds the rest together and makes them perfect. Christ's peace must reign in your hearts . . . Let the word of Christ, rich as it is, dwell in you. In wisdom made perfect, instruct and admonish one another. . . . Whatever you do, whether in speech or in action, do it in the name of the Lord Jesus" (Col. 3: 12-17).

Beyond the personal qualities and demeanor of the educator, there are three other elements that contribute to a climate for conversion: (1) reflection and moral dialogue; (2) the school handbook as a tool for mission effectiveness; and, (3) policies that reflect the core principles of gospel conversion. Each element adds to the dimension of instruction in virtue.

Reflection and Moral Dialogue

Hudson discussed correction as a teachable moment that invites *"moral dialogue,"*[28] i.e., correction that occurs in the context of an adult-student conversation that:

- makes explicit reference to virtues that are relevant to the situation;
- examines student choices in the light of the tradition, purpose or mission, and the Catholic identity of the school, rather than focusing solely on the letter of the law as expressed in handbook regulations;

- involves the student in naming and justifying the ethical principle(s) that call for conversion; and,
- situates correction within the context of Four R's: reflection, response, restitution, and reconciliation.

Moral dialogue takes time. Correction that consists of a teacher simply calling attention to an infraction and then issuing a demerit slip, detention appointment, or sending a student for a time-out is efficient, it restores order to the classroom, and it establishes the teacher as boss, but it is ineffective for conversion. There are effective uses for such tools as demerit notices and detentions. Demerit notices, like the traffic yellow-caution light, signal to the student and parents that braking now can avoid future disaster. Notice is served in time that a student can remediate and re-focus for success. Usually detention is reserved for serious disruptions like fighting or for accumulated infractions like repeated demerits for missing homework or misbehavior. If, however, they are applied in the absence of moral dialogue, they are reaction rather than response. Thus they are efficient but less effective. It has been said that, *"Not everything faced can be changed, but nothing can be changed until it is faced."*[29] James Baldwin advised, *"You cannot fix what you cannot face."*[30] Reflective questioning of student behavior choices is a potential conversion factor.

Conversion requires that the individual names the behavior that has caused distress, knows why it is a life-blocking behavior, understands what motivated the behavior choice, and recognizes positive ways of dealing with such stress in the future. Only when the student is involved in this kind of reflection can he "own" his behavior and make a positive change. Even after this process the student may not convert or change. Conversion, after all, takes years; the life of St. Augustine provides a cogent example.[31] Conversion will not occur at all without moral dialogue or self-reflection. Teachers, through methods, policies, practices, and personal interaction must teach students how to name, claim, and tame their emotions.

Moral dialogue and self-reflection occurs at all stages of life. Of course, a middle-school student is more able to participate in a dialogue of depth than a child of kindergarten age, but both can participate in the process of self-reflection. For example, a six-year-old can name "smiling face behavior" and "frowning face behavior." Sister Thais Margiotta, IHM, a primary-school teacher from Holy Family School (Harrisburg, PA) has her students divide a paper into four sections and illustrate responses to the following four questions:

- What happened?
- What were the consequences of the action?
- What will you do the next time?
- What will the consequences be next time?

Once children are able express themselves in written language, the same four questions can serve as tools for discursive responses. Some teachers of young children provide a chart of "feeling faces" so that a little one can learn to name the feeling that led to his poor-choice-behavior. Once class discussion and possibly class decoration of the Choose Life concept occurs (see the prologue), children in middle school are capable of naming their behaviors as "life-giving" or "life-blocking." They can explain the "why" behind their choices and outcomes and they can name options for the future. Prior to a discussion with a teacher or administrator, a written reflection is a useful tool for students in grade four and beyond. After completion of such a sheet, discussion may not even be necessary. One teacher created a reflection sheet to use during disciplinary encounters with adolescents. Though vocabulary terms require age-appropriate adjustment, the following questions may serve as a guide. They focus on reflection, response, restitution, and reconciliation.

- What values (virtues) were present or needed during the disciplinary episode?
- How do your choices reflect the purpose or mission of our school, our tradition, our Catholic identity?
- If you had it to do all over again, how could you achieve your goal while acting socially responsible?
- How will you make restitution?
- What will it take for you to experience reconciliation? How can I help that process?

Exercises such as these provide a platform for moral instruction and formation. Christian discipline leads the person to understanding, maturity, and a conversion that is marked by freedom and expressed in terms of responsibility, responsiveness, and self-control.

Two years ago the faculty of St. Joseph School (Auburn, CA), led by principal Joan Walthers, initiated a school-wide program of discipline, which, they reported, achieves these goals. The faculty wanted to develop an approach to discipleship that helped students to assume responsibility for their actions without the use of either reward or punishment. They adapted the work of Marvin Marshall to fit the needs of their school by integrating the gospel values of forgiveness, community, and prayer into his *"The Raise Responsibility System."* The faculty in-serviced themselves through discussion and consideration of Marshall's book, *Discipline Without Stress, Punishments, or Rewards.*[32] Before the program was implemented, the teachers provided an in-service for parents, staff members, and students. As Wathers recalled:

> *"It was necessary for us to keep in mind that a [discipline] program that does not encourage good choices by giving rewards was [a concept] foreign to people. It took some time for staff and parents to become accustomed to the idea of children making good choices because it is the right thing to do and not because they would receive a reward, i.e., sticker, candy, movie, etc. . . . We see the most improvement this year in the seventh and eighth grades."*[33]

How does *"The Raise Responsibility System"* function? In sum, all constituents of the school define, in age-appropriate ways, four categories of behavior. These "A-B-C-D" behaviors are:

- Anarchy;
- Bullying;
- Cooperative; and,
- Democratic.

Students in each homeroom discuss the four terms, giving examples to illustrate their understanding of the words. If a student displays "life-blocking" behaviors once the program has begun the adult merely asks the student, "And that behavior is?" The student then identifies the behavior by its category. Generally, that is enough to drive the point home, re-focus, and re-direct the student. If poor choices increase or if more intervention is needed, the program includes steps that incorporate written self-examination. If "A" or "B" behavior choices escalate, the student is indicating that more intervention is required in order for self-disciplined behavior to result. At that point, the teacher directs the student to make an appointment with the principal to review the situation. The principal provides a pre-appointment sheet that guides moral consideration prior to discussion. This includes God-centered statements that orient students to virtue. These statements can be altered as circumstances warrant. As Walthers concluded: *We are happy with our adapted version of the program. We will probably want to change our essay questions again next year. This will help to keep students, staff, and parents in tune to the program and more proactive in our approach to it.*

Approaches to the development of self-discipline need to be "both/and," i.e., these approaches are *both* about re-directing, addressing misbehavior, moving from correction to conversion *and* about acknowledging life-giving choices when they are demonstrated, not as reward, but as instruction. At St. Joseph School (Auburn, CA), I saw an example of the positive at work. Second-grade student Robert was serving detention. His teacher told him that detention was over and gave him permission to leave the room. Without being told, Robert put his chair on top of his desk. His teacher commented, "Robert, you put your chair up without being told. What behavior was that?" With a look of puzzlement on his face, Robert thought for a moment. He seemed to freeze in space. Then his eyes widened, he slowly raised his face toward the teacher and with a tone of astonishment he responded, "C?" His teacher said, "Yes, Robert. That was a cooperative behavior choice. Thank you very much." The next day Robert was very active in trying to demonstrate cooperation. Identifying positive behavior to a child and expressing respect or appreciation tells the child he is competent to choose and to do good. In effect, it becomes self-motivating.

This adaptation of the Marshall program is only one approach to classroom disciplinary practices. Teachers may devise any number of alternative strategies to address misbehavior and to validate cooperative behavior. Fundamentally, disciplinary correction or formation requires:

- self-reflection
- personal recognition of the root cause of the behavior;
- understanding of positive alternative behavior; and,
- the desire to grow towards one's God-given potential in order to move from misbehavior to compliance to conversion to freedom and joy in living.

Though essential to the process of conversion, self-examination and internal moral dialogue ought not be reserved only for incidents of correction. Regular opportunities for contemplative prayer are helpful. Schools and individual teachers can pursue this goal in a variety of ways. Some school communities assemble for prayer before school, after lunch, or at dismissal and include a period of silence to recall God's presence and to guide an examination of conscience. Other schools sound a chime over the public address system to call all persons in the school to one minute of private, personal prayer. A chime then calls them back to activity. Principal Christa Hansen explained that the practice at her school began as a peace initiative at the time of the Gulf War (1991). The entire school community so valued and reverenced the custom that students asked to continue the practice after the crisis of the war had passed.[34] The Commissioner of Student Affairs rings the chime daily at 11 a.m. No matter which activity is in progress, i.e., a student rally, PE class, test, or student assemblies with professional presenters, when the chime rings, silence reigns for one minute. Practices such as these establish prayer as a priority. Some students experience a school-wide practice of "Blessing the Hour." The practice occurs once every hour. A designated student rings a bell or attracts class attention by some other means, saying something, such as, *"Pardon me, Mr. Neil. Pardon me, Class. It is time to bless the hour. Let us remember that we are in the holy presence of God."* In unison the class responds: *"Let us adore God's divine majesty.*

Glory be to the Father and to the Son and to the Holy Spirit. As it was in the beginning, is now, and ever shall be, world without end. Amen." Without any further comment class activity resumes at the point that it was interrupted when the student announcement occurred.

Using six-inch tracing letters, eighth-grade teacher Julie Thompson (Holy Spirit School, Fairfield, CA) created a classroom banner with the phrase, *"Let us remember that we are in the holy presence of God."* When the class needs to refocus, she merely points to the banner. Many teachers practice the custom of pausing at the sound of emergency sirens and praying for the victims of the emergency. For instance, at the sound of a fire engine, one class prays aloud, *"Jesus, Mary and Joseph, save souls!"* Another class prays: *"O God, we beseech you to help your servants whom you have redeemed with your precious blood."*

Practices such as these become traditions that define "Catholic School" in the hearts of students. Such practices flavor the educational experience and enflesh the meaning of "Catholic Identity." Some elements of Catholic identity occur at intervals throughout the year; others are daily occurrences. In every instance, these practices cultivate a culture of discipline.

The School Handbook as a Tool for Mission Effectiveness

Ideally, the school handbook is an effective tool in the process of discipleship. The overarching goal of its defined policies, procedures, and actions is to bring students into deeper relationship with Christ, self, and others. Thus the focus of the handbook is both personal growth and the building of faith community.

The school handbook should answer the following questions:
- What is the purpose of your particular Catholic school?
- What is stated in your Mission Statement?
- Can you, the school professional, now repeat the wording of your mission statement?
- Can the students in your school frame the mission statement in their own vocabulary?

If teachers and administrators are able to express the mission of the school, it is likely that the mission is also referenced in conversation, direction, and correction. This is what Cook refers to as *"continuous referencing,"* which he defined as follows: *"As architects of Catholic culture, it is incumbent upon Catholic educational leaders to keep core values and the mission statement in front of their school communities."*[35]

The mission statement, which articulates the purpose of the school, serves as the center out of which principles flow as expressions of a unifying goal. This goal is the fostering of right relationship with God, self, and others. Each principle includes policies and procedures that "unpack" its meaning and reveal the ways in which the purpose of the school is achieved. Rather than reading the contents of the handbook as a list of arbitrary "do's and don'ts," the specifics of the handbook "make sense" because of their relation to the purpose of the school as expressed in its mission statement.

Student discipline formation is nurtured when both school policies and individual teacher management practices reflect the purpose of the school, its values, and the ways in which people are to interact in order to be faithful to the mission statement and effective in its formation. For example, if the school mission statement expresses the goal of accepting all persons as images of God who are called upon to develop their infinite potential, this would be followed by a principle expressing the dignity of each human person. For example, the following synthesis statement based upon key elements of Catholic social teaching that were expressed by the United States Conference of Catholic Bishops provides an example of such a principle:

> *All people are created in the image and likeness of God. . . . People do not lose their dignity because of disability, poverty, age, gender, lack of success or race. . . . We believe that every person is precious and that people are more important than things.* [36]

A school handbook that is structured to move from mission statement to core principles to specific practices is a tool for mission effectiveness and a reliable guide to the development of self-discipline because it is instructive. It distinguishes among various behaviors. It is assertive in promoting a Gospel mindset and social responsibility in students. The inspirational and formative capability of the school mission statement cannot be underestimated. Cook has summarized it well:

> "A Catholic school's mission statement, then, defines, inspires, and guides the school community in all it does. The Catholic school's identity, inspiration, and destiny – as expressed in a mission statement – must then be explicitly connected to Christ and the Gospel (National Conference of Catholic Bishops, 1972, #155). When mission statements truly drive the schooling enterprise, learning activities and outcomes will look very different."[37]

Imagine, for instance, using the school handbook as a vehicle with which to apply the principles of Catholic social teaching. Specific practices advocated for or discouraged in a Catholic school can be understood within the context of one or more of the principles of Catholic social teaching. **Table 3** offers an outline of seven principles and suggests related life-giving expressions and life-blocking behaviors that are often matters of discussion within a school community. This table represents a synthesis[38] and illustrates the possibility of coordinating the mission statement, core principles, and specific practices into a document that can be an aid in the formation and information that cultivates discipleship.

TABLE 3
THE RELATIONSHIP BETWEEN CATHOLIC SOCIAL TEACHING AND SCHOOL DISCIPLINE ISSUES

Principle	Life-Giving Expressions	Life-Blocking Behaviors
• **Sacredness of Life and Dignity of the Human Person** *We believe that every person is precious, that people are more important than things, and that the measure of every institution is whether it threatens or enhances the life and dignity of the human person.*	Recognize the dignity of each person. Respect innate goodness and dignity. Celebrate gifts and talents. Foster growth towards potential. Safeguard the gift of life. Foster mutual respect.	Inadequate academic effort Cheating Abuse: Physical or Emotional Substance abuse Hurtful teasing Harassing Fighting

• **Call to Family, Community, Participation, Common Good** *We believe people have a right and a duty to participate in society, seeking together the common good and well-being of all, especially the poor and vulnerable*	Build community.Promote the common good.Participate in class & activities. Wear uniform with pride. Contribute to a safe learning environment. Practice responsibility & accountability. Preserve the reputation of the school.	Name calling Bullying Weapons Illegal substances Tampering with safety equipment
• **Rights and Responsibilities of the Human Person** *Every person has a fundamental right to life and a right to those things required for human decency. Corresponding to these rights are duties and responsibilities — to one another, to our families, and to the larger society.*	Students do have rights, but they do not have the right to interfere with the rights or the education of others. All students have a right and responsibility to participate in the learning community. Duty to make restitution after violating rights, i.e., detention, suspension, dismissal from events.	Misbehavior Disrupting class Disregarding the expectations of teacher or School Handbook
• **Option for the Poor and Vulnerable** *In a society marred by deepening divisions between rich and poor, our tradition recalls the story of the Last Judgment (Mt 25:31-46) and instructs us to put the needs of the poor and vulnerable first.*	Students who are struggling: academically, emotionally, socially, at home, etc. Value uniform code to help students recognize each another for who they are, not what they wear.	Elitism Cliques Treating maintenance persons as inferior or as servants
• **Dignity of Work and the Rights of Workers** *If the dignity of work is to be protected, then the basic rights of workers must be respected — the right to productive work, to decent and fair wages, to organize*	Education is inherent to dignity. Learning is the vocation of students. Learning environment is students' work place. Maintenance personnel share equal dignity.	Disrespectful or distracting behavior. Demonstrating an attitude of "entitlement"; expecting others to pick up after you

and join unions, to private property, and to economic initiative.		
• **Solidarity of the Human Family** *We are our brothers' and sisters' keepers, wherever they live. Learning to practice the virtue of solidarity means learning that "loving our neighbor" has global dimensions in an interdependent world.*	Respect and inclusion regardless of race, gender, orientation, nationality, religion	Slurs: racial, religious, ethnic, gender, or sexual orientation
• **Care for Creation** *We are called to protect people and the planet, living our faith in relationship with all of God's creation. This environmental challenge has fundamental moral and ethical dimensions that cannot be ignored.*	Stewardship for environment and materials. Respectful and responsible for school building, grounds, equipment	Destruction or damage to property Expecting others to clean up after you.

School Policies that reflect Core Principles of Gospel Conversion

A culture of self-discipline flourishes in an atmosphere that integrates school life with the Gospel of Jesus and the Jesus of the Gospels. The foundation for conversion is rooted in the interconnection of four fundamental Gospel values: justice, redemption, restitution, and reconciliation.

Issues of justice are often implicit in student complaints, e.g., "It's not fair!" "You pick on me!" "Other kids don't have to do it." "You play favorites!" Justice is an essential element for conversion. Children need to believe that they are treated respectfully and justly before they can acknowledge faults or wrongdoing. Certainly, the Catholic educator and his or her actions must be characterized by the four cardinal virtues (prudence, justice, fortitude, and temperance), but it is injustice that most quickly blocks the spirit of conversion. As the *Catechism of the Catholic Church* says:

"Justice is the moral virtue that consists in the constant and firm will to give their due to God an neighbor. Justice toward God is called 'the virtue of religion.' Justice toward men disposes one to respect the rights of each and to establish in human relationships the harmony that promotes equity with regard to persons and to the common good. The just man, often mentioned in the Sacred Scriptures, is distinguished by habitual right thinking and the uprightness of his conduct toward his neighbor. 'You shall not be partial to the poor or defer to the great, but in righteousness shall you judge your neighbor. (Lev.19:15; #1807).'"

Justice is inherently communal: it calls people to apprehend their connection to others, to be responsible to them and for them, to let the needs of others matter, and to seek the common good. Justice is the virtue of just dealing, right action, and fair treatment, despite personal preference, mood, or prejudice. Justice strives to give others their due. M. McCarty has summarized it this way:

"The principles of equality and justice also flow from concern for human welfare and entitle everyone to fair treatment. The rights given to one of us must be given to all of us in the same situation or circumstances. In practice, treating others as we'd like to be treated means that we must respect and protect others' rights as we'd like our rights to be respected and safeguarded. If we have the opportunity to do or obtain something, then everyone in the same circumstances should have that opportunity. We shouldn't restrict, limit, or penalize others in ways we'd consider unjust if we were in the same situation. Everyone is entitled to just and equal opportunities. . . . Justice is the very least we can do if we claim to follow Jesus. Justice and equality are another way of saying, 'Treat others as you want them to treat you.' Christianity and democracy both maintain that if we're to accept justice and equality as our rights, then we must also see that they are extended to others."[39]

A consideration of the challenge of justice suggests the following kinds of questions to Catholic educators:

- How consistently does relationship characterize my dealings with all students?
- How consistently do I apply the same standard and disposition evenly to all students regardless of rank,

privilege, or positions of power within the school/parish community?

- How consistently do I demonstrate respect the dignity of each child?
- How consistently do I honor the rights of each child?
- How vigilant am I in balancing the common good with care for each student, especially the helpless, innocent, oppressed or neediest students?
- How consistently do I give to the child who practices annoying behaviors the same attention, patience, and opportunity that I extend to less needy students?
- How proactive am I in protecting unpopular students from becoming victims of injustice or inequality?
- How creative am I in working toward unity and harmony rather than dissension?
- How actively do I work to replace discriminatory attitudes with attitudes of community?
- How faithful am I in treating all others as I would want to be treated or as I would want my child, my niece, nephew or friend to be treated?

Redemption

Redemption is the central message of the Gospel. The Son of God coexisted with the Father and the Spirit before there was a Bethlehem. And yet, "in the fullness of time" (Gal. 4:4), the Son of God became flesh, he was named Jesus, and dwelled among humanity (Jn. 1:1-11). Since humanity has been damaged by sin, the Son of God came to earth in order to redeem humanity, to show the way to the Father, and to restore humanity to friendship with God. Catholics rejoice in the mystery of the Incarnation and celebrate redemption in every Eucharistic liturgy. Eucharistic Prayer IV proclaims salvation history:

"Father, we acknowledge your greatness: all your actions show your wisdom and love. You formed man in your own likeness and set him over the whole world to serve you, his creator, and to rule over all creatures. *Even when he disobeyed you and lost your friendship you did not abandon him to the power of death, but helped all men to seek and find you. Again and again you offered a covenant to man*, and through the prophets taught him to hope for salvation. Father, you so loved the world that in the fullness of time you sent your only son to be our Savior. He was conceived through the power of the Holy Spirit, and born of the Virgin Mary, a man like us in all things but sin. *To the poor he proclaimed the good news of salvation, to prisoners, freedom, and to those in sorrow, joy.* In fulfillment of your will he gave himself up to death; but by rising from the dead, *he destroyed death and restored life.* And that we might live no longer for ourselves but for him, he sent the Holy Spirit from you, Father, as the first gift to those who believe, to complete his work on earth and bring us the fullness of grace. . ." (italics mine).[40]

Consider that we would never have met Christ or learned about God as Father, Son and Spirit, except for the sin of Adam and Eve. Jesus came in response to their sin! That is why the *Exsultet* of the Easter Vigil liturgy proclaims: *"Oh, happy fault! Oh, necessary sin of Adam."* This is not to say that sin is a good to be sought! Sin is a break in our relationship with God and an estrangement from God, self, or others. Sin causes us to shut down and to shut out Jesus and others. No, the Easter *Exsultet* does not encourage sin. It affirms that nothing is beyond the power of God to redeem. Sin can actually become a steppingstone in spiritual development if we invite Jesus to transform it and us! The life-long process of transformation is easily illustrated to students by demonstrating a transformer toy that changes its identity merely by re-configuring the position of its pieces. All pieces are used; none are discarded. A dinosaur can take the shape of a space ship and, with the grace of God, a sinner can become a saint! Jesus invites us to place all that we are into his hands: our strengths, weaknesses, virtues, vices, the acceptable parts of our personalities and choices as well as the unacceptable features that we reject or deny. . We come to learn from experience that *"Nothing is impossible for God"* (Lk. 1:37) and that *"I can do all things in him who strengthens me"* (Phil. 4:13).

Christ redeems! Jesus, who was like us in all things but sin (Heb. 4:15), continually offers us another chance and through forgiveness he makes possible renewed relationship with God and life everlasting. Though we do not deserve and cannot earn restoration, God gifts us with renewed relationship. This is a mystery of faith that teachers proclaim to students through words, but more importantly through actions.

What has this to do with correction and conversion? The redemptive mission of Jesus has everything to do with the way people should approach correction and self-discipline. With Jesus, the Catholic school educator is called to proclaim and to practice the good news of Jesus. Conversion follows experiences of redemption: new chances, renewed trust, an opportunity to be restored to integrity, respect, and friendship. For example, instance, when Jesus invited himself to dine with Zaccheus, the tax collector, Zaccheus responded with delight and declared to the public his change of heart and plans for restitution (Lk. 19: 1-10). Zaccheus illustrated metànoia, the process of reversing one's thinking, feeling, and acting to manifest through concrete actions an inner mental change. Conversion is more likely for student who experiences redemption in a teacher-student encounter. In the words of Pope Paul VI in *Paenitemini*:

> *"We must approach the kingdom of Christ through metànoia and only in this way, which means through a profound change of the whole man as a result of which he begins to think, judge, and arrange his whole life under the impulse of that holiness and charity of God which have been manifested and fully imparted to us last of all in the Son."*[41]

When a student gets into trouble, is he/she abandoned for the rest of the year or is new life offered? Through their experience of correction students should realize that sins and mistakes are like bricks: they can be used to build a wall or a bridge. Actually, character is shaped by the way we respond to our failures. A personal anecdote illustrates this point. When I was an eighth-grade student, I had a touching experience of redemption that made all the difference to me and to the shaping of my soul. I offer it to you that it may affirm or instruct your beliefs about discipline and discipleship. It is a story that says little about me but much about a Catholic educator whose effort to live true to the spirit of Jesus had a formative effect on a child.

During a Friday lunchtime recess when all children were required to be in the school yard, my teacher, Sr. Marie Cornelia, IHM, singled me out to do a task. She gave me her key ring and told me to take a girl friend with me to decorate the back of the classroom with student book reports. That was a distinct honor and trust. Delightedly my friend and I set off to accomplish the task. While I was in the back of the room attending to my charge, my friend was inspecting Sister's desk, a definite "no-no"! She found there a Civics test and was excited with her find since we were scheduled for a test in the afternoon session. Civics was not my strong suit; nor was it hers. She said, "Pat, here is the Civics test. Do you want to see it?" I was able to say, "No, thanks!" and I continued my decorating activity. A second time my friend said, "I'll make a copy of the answers for you". Again I said, "No, thank you". In a few minutes my friend appeared at my side and handed me a personal copy of the answers. I put them into my pocket. I offer this as an explanation—not an excuse! My friend gave me the unsolicited answers. I did not have to take them and I certainly did not have to use them. That afternoon, for the first time in my life, I cheated! I used the slip of paper to fill in the answers on my test.

The weekend passed and Monday arrived. Again I was at lunchtime recess when Sister beckoned me to her side. When I met with her she asked: "Patricia, is there something that you need to tell me?" I said, "No, Sister." She permitted a pregnant pause and then, with eye contact that seemed to bore through my soul she asked with slow deliberation, "Patricia, are you sure that there is not something that you need to tell me?" Quite frankly, I thought I would be physically sick on the spot! The Spirit offered me the grace of integrity and the strength to be truthful and to face the music. I accepted the grace. I replied, "Yes, Sister. I cheated on my Civics test". They were the hardest words that I ever spoke to this teacher whom I respected so much and whose respect I had appreciated. She replied, "Yes, Patricia. I know that you cheated and I will tell you how. You found a civics test on my desk and you copied the answers onto your test. Patricia, you failed your test. You usually do good work and when I saw your test it puzzled me. So I looked into the situation and found that your answers matched the paper that was on my desk. But, Patricia, that paper was not the test!" (How bright was I, really?)

I do not remember anything that followed that schoolyard interview but I certainly remember how poorly I felt about myself and how sorry I felt that I broke trust with this woman whose opinion mattered to me. Two or three weeks went by. Sister never referred back to the situation; nor did she treat me any differently than what I knew of her before my fall from grace. Regardless, I felt the weight of my sin. I experienced what it was to lose respect for myself and the respect of someone whom I admired, all for a test grade. Then one lunchtime afternoon Sister called me over to her. When I arrived she removed her key ring from her cincture, handed me her keys, and asked me to do a job for her in the classroom.

This was a moment of redemption. I knew I did not deserve her forgiveness or respect and, yet, Sister offered me a fresh start as though nothing had come between us. I learned more from her gesture than sermons or religious instruction periods could convey. I learned mercy, forgiveness, and integrity. I learned how healing it was to be restored to friendship and welcomed back into community. I experienced redemption and a chance to make all things new!

There are two other major lessons contained in this story that can aid in the correction of students. First, when a teacher already knows the truth, a confession should not be forced. Initially, children are tempted to lie. They are embarrassed at being found out. They worry about what people think of them and they are fearful of the consequences of their lie. Instinctively, Sister Marie Cornelia knew about the lie, but rather than asking me to tell her how I cheated, she told me. She began the conversation by asking, *"Patricia, is there something that you need to tell me?"* She made it possible for me to exercise autonomy and personal accountability and enabled me to break the cycle of dishonesty on my own and take a step to restoring self-respect. Had I not admitted my sin and, instead, held fast to my "no" answer, Sister would still have laid out the scenario before me, but I would have experienced deeper shame, not relief or self-respect. Bishop Sheen once said, *"It is easier to create faith than to restore it."* Once faith or personal trust is broken, truth is essential to the process of restoration. Children should understand this in order to understand why lying is harmful. It breaks trust and without trust there is no relationship. The second lesson suggested in this story is one of perspective. Children lack the perspective that comes with experience. Compassion extends perspective to students: compel them encounter a poor choice, its effects, and its consequences, and then put all of these away in favor of choosing life. In other words, as discussed earlier, let a mistake or even a sin become a steppingstone to development, not the boulder that seals a tomb. Redemption means that there is still a chance for love.

Reflection on the mystery of Redemption, as expressed in Eucharistic Prayer IV, suggests the following questions to Catholic educators:

- *"Even when he disobeyed you and lost your friendship you did not abandon him to the power of death, but helped all men to seek and find you."*[42]

  Through correction and after correction, do I help students to return to relationship, community, and friendship or are they doomed to isolation?

- *"To the poor he proclaimed the good news of salvation, to prisoners, freedom, and to those in sorrow, joy."*

  Do I attempt to meet students where they are and tailor my correction to their need and in proportion to their offense?

- *"He destroyed death and restored life."*

  When I correct wrongdoing, am I motivated by a spirit of destruction, or a spirit of resurrection?

  When confronting the wrongdoer, do I speak the truth in love, or do I intend my words to sting, punish, and shame?

Restitution

Restitution is often conceived in material terms as a return of property or goods to the rightful owner, or financial compensation for loss or damage, as illustrated by P.J. Wadell's definition:

> *"Restitution is the return of or repayment for something stolen from another. Restitution is a moral obligation of justice; it is a way of repairing whatever damage or loss another person or group has suffered on account of one's crime. Sometimes it is impossible to return exactly what has been taken. In such cases something of the same value must be substituted. If we have stolen something, it is not enough just to be sorry. We must in justice pay back what we have taken."*[43]

Indeed, restitution has a material aspect, but this definition should include restitution as the re-establishment of right relations after a break in relationship, or, as Paul VI expressed it in *The Duty of Peace*: "*Reconciliation demands the normalization of our relations with our neighbor.*"[44] Recall that Jesus said, "*If you bring your gift to the altar and there recall that your brother has anything against you, leave your gift . . . go first to be reconciled with your brother, and then come and offer your gift* (Mt. 5: 23-25)." Moral living includes healing a conflict, making amends for any damage that our sin has caused to another person, asking forgiveness of someone we have injured, and making things right again.[45] B. Coloroso defines reconciliation as "*the process of healing with the person you have harmed.*"[46] Reconciliation and restitution are components of moral theology. Integral to conversion is the acknowledgement that certain choices have had a negative relationship with another individual or the community. The offender needs to acknowledge the effects of his or her choices and then work toward healing and repairing the damage. In *Brotherly Reconciliation*, Pope Paul VI taught that relational restitution means "*forgiving and forgetting offenses, setting up again peaceful and friendly relations, resuming conversation and trust. . . .*"[47] Healing can be achieved in a number of ways: with a sincere apology, befriending the offended person, correcting a lie, or attempting to restore the damaged reputation of another. On these occasions Catholic educators can invite the student to decide on the way(s) he or she will make restitution.

Kohn cites an example of a teacher-led discussion aimed at anticipating misbehavior and involving the class community in the solution:

"Begin by asking this question (adapting it as necessary to the students' developmental level): 'What if, some time this year, you found yourself acting in a way you weren't proud of? Suppose you hurt someone's feelings, or did something even worse. How would you want us, the rest of the community, to help you then?' After everyone has reflected privately on this question, and perhaps discussed it, pose the follow-up question: 'What if someone else acted that way? How could we help that person?' . . .

This thought experiment represents nothing short of a revolution in thinking about classroom problems. Actions that would normally be defined as misbehavior—and therefore as requiring discipline—are reconstrued as signs that somebody needs help. If a student had trouble with long division, after all, we would naturally want to help him understand the procedure (and its rationale), rather than seeking to punish him. So if a student instead had trouble, say, controlling her temper, our response again ought to be 'How can we help?'—not 'What consequence should you suffer?' We should ask, in other words, 'What can we do for you?'—not 'What can we do to you?' (italics in original)

It works both ways, really: The best choice for dealing with problems, or for preventing their occurrence in the first place, is to invoke the support and ideas of the community. And the best choice for building a community may be to take on this sort of challenge together."[48]

These questions can be followed with others that deal with reconciliation: i.e., "What could the student do to make amends for her behavior?" "What kinds of activities would repair the damage done?" "What might it take to restore the student to right relations with the person or class who was offended?"

Reconciliation

Reconciliation completes the cycle of forgiveness. To be reconciled is to be called back to life. It is the restoration of a relationship as though the break had never occurred. The offense is not forgotten, but it is not a barrier to future relationship. McCarty offers helpful advice here:

> "Forgiveness requires even more of us. It may mean standing up to the person, letting the offender know that the wrongful behavior won't be tolerated. It might mean removing people from circumstances that would tempt them to repeat the offense. It may require protecting oneself and others from again being victimized. It might mean benching a star athlete, impeaching an official, or refusing to buy the musician's recordings or see the actor's films."[49]

Forgiveness does not mean that one agrees with a wrong, or that it is not important. Rather, forgiveness means that a person is treated with the same respect that others want for themselves. In reconciliation persons are given another chance, an opportunity to prove themselves and improve, to change and make things different. This is not easy. It calls for compassion, patience, and Christ-likeness. As Pope Paul VI said in his *World Day of Peace Address*: "*Reconciling love is not weakness, is not cowardice: it demands strong, noble and generous, sometimes heroic feelings: it calls for the overcoming of oneself rather than of one's enemy. . . . In reality, reconciling love will be the patient, wise art of peace, of wishing well to another, of living together as brothers [and sisters] after the example of Christ and with the strength of heart modeled on his.*"[50] If educators can be an experience of Christ for students, conversion becomes possible.

Consideration of the gift of reconciliation suggests the following questions to Catholic educators:

- What is my pattern of correction?
- Do I offer opportunities for reconciliation?
- Do I initiate conversation at a neutral time?
- Do I invite the student the a renewed relationship?
- Do I create situations that allow the student to have both leadership and inclusion?

Conversion In the Context of Community

Discipleship flourishes in community. In a context of relationships, students can apprehend disciplinary policies and procedures as moral standards to which they aspire, rather than as limits to be endured or ignored. Students who regard themselves as part of a community honor the ideas, ideals, and values of the communal "we" and express partnership in both words and deeds. Students who experience community are emotionally connected to the common good and common purpose. They are bound by relationships, shared values, and what it means to be members of a particular class or school. Environment and ritual also reveals the goals of welcome and inclusion. Indeed, the communal dimension of school is a crucial element in the process of correction and conversion. It is a dimension that relies heavily, though certainly not solely, on Catholic educators. As the bishops said:

"Before concluding, we should like to dwell briefly on the climate and role of the educating community, which is constituted by the interaction and collaboration of its various components: students, parents, teachers, directors and non-teaching staff. Attention is rightly given to the importance of the relations existing among all those who make up the educating community. During childhood and adolescence a student needs to experience personal relations with outstanding educators, and what is taught has greater influence on the student's formation when placed in a context of personal involvement, genuine reciprocity, coherence of attitudes, lifestyles and day-to-day behavior. While respecting individual roles, the community dimension should be fostered, since it is one of the most enriching developments for the contemporary school. It is also helpful to bear in mind, in harmony with the Second Vatican Council, that this community dimension in the Catholic school is not a merely sociological category; it has theological foundation as well. The educating community, taken as a whole, is thus called to further the objective of a school as a place of complete formation through interpersonal relations (#18).

In the Catholic school, 'prime responsibility for creating this unique Christian school climate rests with the teachers, as individuals and as a community.' Teaching has an extraordinary moral depth and is one of man's most excellent and creative activities, for the teacher does not write on inanimate material, but on the very spirits of human beings. The personal relations between the teacher and the students, therefore, assume an enormous importance and are not limited simply to giving and taking. Moreover, we must remember that teachers and educators fulfill a specific Christian vocation and share an equally specific participation in the mission of the Church, to the extent that 'it depends chiefly on them whether the Catholic school achieves its purpose.' "[51]

Though crucial to community, building a climate of community involves more than simply the teacher-student relationship. Kohn suggests four levels of endeavor: *". . . (1) strengthening the adult's relationship with each student; (2) building students' connections with each other, one dyad at a time; (3) providing for numerous classwide and schoolwide activities in which students work together toward a common end; and (4) weaving the goal of community through academic instruction."*[52] Each aspect invites consideration and strategic planning. Readers will find an expanded discussion in the succeeding chapters of this book.

A student who recognizes that he or she is situated within the context of community is more likely to accept the grace of conversion, to become more loving, to develop self-respect and respect for the community and to grow as a contributing member of that community. Although Catholic educators want to offer community, compassion, forgiveness, and an opportunity for restitution as the pattern of interacting with students, this does not mean that suspension, expulsion, or zero-tolerance policies have no place. Hudson explained it well when he suggested that community has an organic nature.[53] He likened some behavior choices to cancer that are first treated with radiation or chemotherapy before radical surgery. Surgery is the last resort. A part of the body is cut off in order to save the rest of the body. When community values or safety are at risk, or when a student action has a serious negative effect on the community, the student may be placed outside the school community. The spirit of justice, redemption, restitution, and reconciliation suggests that the following are important: (1) due process, (2) speaking truthfully in love; (3) leading the student to see the cause and effect of his or her choices both personally and communally; (4) encouraging restitution that leads the student to regain self-respect; (5) offering continued prayerful support as well as practical help in situating the student in another school, therapy program, or treatment center, and, (6) inviting the student to return to the school community after a successful semester or year elsewhere.[54]

In his jubilee year apostolic letter , *Novo Millennio Ineunte (At the Beginning of the New Millennium),* John Paul II directed all Christians to make community their fundamental objective:

> ". . . We need to **promote a spirituality of communion**, making it the guiding principle of education wherever individuals and Christians are formed. . .

> "A spirituality of communion indicates above all the heart's contemplation of the mystery of the Trinity dwelling in us, and whose light we must also be able to see on the face of the brothers and sisters around us.

> A spirituality of communion also means an ability to think of our brothers and sisters in faith within the profound unity of the Mystical Body, and therefore as 'those who are a part of me.' This makes us able to share their joys and sufferings, to sense their desires and attend to their needs, to offer them deep and genuine friendship.

> A spirituality of communion implies also the ability to see what is positive in others, to welcome it and prize it as a gift from God; not only as a gift for the brother or sister who has received it directly, but also as a 'gift for me.'

> A spirituality of communion means, finally, to know how to 'make room' for our brothers and sisters, bearing 'each other's burdens' (Gal. 6:2) and resisting the selfish temptations which constantly beset us and provoke competition, careerism, distrust, and jealousy.

Let us have no illusions: unless we follow this spiritual path, external structures of communion will serve very little purpose. They would become mechanisms without a soul, 'masks' of communion rather than its means of expression and growth." [55]

In this passage, John Paul II provides guidance for building and sustaining a culture of community:

- finding Christ in one another
- thinking of others as extensions of oneself
- doing for others what I would want for myself
- honoring the joys and sorrows of another
- relating in genuine friendship
- affirming the efforts and potential of others
- viewing others as gifts
- being inclusive and inviting
- practicing tolerance and mutual support
- resisting selfishness

CHAPTER TWO

Self-Discipline: More Caught than Taught!

The Vocation of Teachers is Indispensable to Discipleship

The effort to bring another to recognize the love of God that is revealed in and through Jesus is evangelization, the perennial mission of the Catholic Church. Discipleship begins with recognition of the love of God, moves to response, and is completed with imitation of Jesus. Evangelization and discipleship comprise the bipartite vocation of Catholic educators. This desire to lead students to Jesus is the grace of a vocation that differentiates Catholic educators from others. The mission to make a difference in children is *an issue of faith, an accurate indicator of our faith in Christ and his love for us.*[56] Catholic educators resonate with the message of St. Paul: *"The love of Christ impels us"* (2 Cor. 5:14), because Catholic educators are, first of all, people of faith. Formation is the primary motive for working in a Catholic school. Impelled by this vocation, teachers model discipleship to their students. They, in turn, "catch" the spirit of self-discipline through observation and personal interaction, rather than coercion.

Teachers who share this vocation exude energy and enthusiasm. Despite typical pressures and challenges, disappointments and setbacks that characterize a day or a season, the teacher is hope-filled and resilient. In the midst of stress or criticism, trust in God leads the educator to say with St. Paul:

"We know that affliction makes for endurance, and endurance for tested virtue, and tested virtue for hope" (Rom. 5:3-4). " We are afflicted in every way possible, but we are not crushed; full of doubts, we never despair. We are persecuted but never abandoned; we are struck down but never destroyed. . . . We have that spirit of faith of which the Scripture says, 'Because I believed, I spoke out.' We believe and so we speak . . ." (2 Cor. 4: 8-13).

As John Paul II has affirmed: *"The Church serves the kingdom by spreading throughout the world the 'gospel values' which are an expression of the kingdom and which help people to accept God's plan."*[57] Catholic educators serve God's kingdom by weaving gospel values into the whole of the school day, values which define the kingdom and which help students to accept God's plan for them. This is possible only by responding to the grace of vocation. In short, through the witness of their lives, Catholic educators promote Christ-like behavior during challenging times. Their witness supports or augments the efforts of parents whose primary responsibility it is to foster the soulful formation of children. Is there any more vital vocation than that of the Catholic School educator?

Contemporary leaders in Catholic education have affirmed the positive power of vocation, the passion that is characteristic of vocation, and the characteristics that mark a Catholic school teacher who perceives teaching to be a vocation rather than a job. The following quotations, taken from a series of articles in *Momentum*, highlight the different aspects of the vocation of Catholic educators.

Robert Kealey, the former Executive Director for Elementary Schools at NCEA, has said:

"Our personal sanctification as Catholic educators comes from how faithful we are as religious, priest, spouse, parent, or single person. Intimately connected to that vocation is how faithful we are in our ministry. We find Christ in the person of those we teach. . . . We share our personal experiences of Christ with our students when the teachable moment arises."[58]

Sister Carol Cimino, Executive Director of the Catholic School Administrators Association of New York State, notes that a teacher's actions speak more powerfully than words:

> ". . . students need to experience the wonderful self-giving of the adults around them. What more inspiring example than the teacher who has a sense of his or her vocation as a teacher? The influence of the teacher as model of what it means to be an adult Christian with a personal and an institutional ministry gives testimony to St. Francis of Assisi's admonition: 'Preach the Gospel at all times; once in awhile, use words.'"[59]

Vocation is dynamic. A.D. Roach, retired school superintendent of the Archdiocese of Boston and now a missionary in Chile, has expressed the need for personal recognition of vocation and continued growth in responding wholeheartedly to the call:

> "From my perspective, the professional preparation of teachers is a given. However, for a Catholic school educator to own that her or she has a specific vocation is essential, and must be nurtured within each school community. Just as Jesus grew in knowledge of His vocation, teachers grow in their understanding of the ministerial call and its accompanying responsibilities. This ownership occurs when the Catholic school educator is able to define, strengthen, and articulate those enduring values, beliefs, and cultural strands that give the school its unique identity."[60]

Superintendent Mary McDonald has captured the spirit of the New Evangelization in this way:

> "We teach the children, not because they are Catholic, but because we are (italics in original). That is our vocation. Catholic education is a mission in our Church and the teachers in the Catholic schools are the missionaries of the new millennium. . . . But teaching in a Catholic school is not just a job, it is a vocation. It is a call by God to do His work."[61]

Principal Patricia McNamee reflects on the dynamic of call, response, and effect in this way:

"Recognizing the talents with which we are blessed and using these talents to build the Kingdom of God is, I believe, a most telling definition of vocation. I believe that vocation is for each person as unique as one's fingerprints. I believe also that God gives to each of us the grace and the skill to respond to His call. . . . I believe that it is only in responding to the sanctity of each person and the significance of each challenge we encounter that we can answer our call and feel fulfilled, satisfied, productive, and joyful."[62]

These leaders represent years of experience in living out the cyclical dynamic of vocation: call, response, and effect. They know that vocation is a gift of God, a call by God first to creation, then to life *in* Christ, to relationship *with* Christ, and to the service *of* Christ. Vocation is given expression in ministry and manifests as aspect of God to the world. Catholic educators are called to be a sign of God to people. To the extent that they are, they contribute to the development of discipleship in their students. Frederick Buechner expressed well the animating spirit of vocation:

"Go now, into the world in peace, and know how much an old world needs your spirit and hope. Recognize there are words of truth that will never be spoken unless you speak them and deeds of compassion and courage that will never be done unless you do them. Never mistake success for victory or failure for defeat. Know that you were not created for happiness but for joy, and joy is to them alone who, sometimes with tears in their eyes, commit themselves in love to God and to their brothers and sisters."[63]

The intentional response of a teacher to the grace of vocation is the indispensable element in Catholic education. It is the factor that most distinguishes a school that is rooted in a faith-tradition. Whether or not a Catholic school achieves its purpose depends, to a great extent, on the Catholic character of its teachers, expressed in both word and example. In the *Declaration on Christian Education*, the Fathers of the Second Vatican Council identified teachers as crucial to the mission of evangelization:

" But let teachers realize that to the greatest possible extent they determine whether the Catholic school can bring its goals and undertakings to fruition. . . . Bound by charity to one another and to their students, and penetrated by an apostolic spirit, let them give witness to Christ, the unique Teacher, by their lives as well as by their teachings" (#8).

Acknowledgement of the essential role of teachers in the ministry of formation has been a recurrent theme in post-Vatican II Church documents. The effect of the personality and virtue of the teacher on the evangelization of students is of priceless value and was reaffirmed by the Congregation for Catholic Education:

"The achievement of this specific aim of the Catholic school depends not so much on subject matter or methodology as on the people who work there. The extent to which the Christian message is transmitted through education depends to a very great extent on the teachers. The integration of culture and faith is mediated by the other integration of faith and life in the person of the teacher. The nobility of the task to which teachers are called demands that, in imitation of Christ, the only Teacher, they reveal the Christian message not only by word but also by every gesture of their behavior. This is what makes the difference between a school whose education is permeated by the Christian spirit and one in which religion is only regarded as an academic subject like any other."[64]

Academic preparation and on-going participation in curriculum development, teaching practices, technology, etc., are characteristics of effective teachers, but the quality of faith of teachers is the crucial credential. Who we are speaks more effectively than words can ever do! Teachers in a Catholic school are called to an "otherworldly" standard. John Convey suggests that Catholic educators must meet three standards beyond their professional development:

1. Permeate the curriculum and classroom with Gospel values.

". . .teachers must be witnesses to the faith, by being committed to helping their students develop Christian beliefs and values (Congregation

for Catholic Education, 1982, #29) and by being willing to model for their students 'how these beliefs and values shape and inform spiritual, moral, and lifestyle choices'(Bensen & Guerra, 1985, p.2). Catholic school teachers must constantly be alert for opportunities to initiate the appropriate dialogue between culture and faith (Congregation for Catholic Education, 1982, #29)."

2. Be a faithful witness of what you teach.

". . . in addition to being witnesses by the way they teach, teachers in Catholic schools must provide in the conduct of their daily lives a witness to the beliefs and values that they teach (Congregation for Catholic Education, 1982, #32). Students should see in their teachers Christian attitudes and behaviors. Catholic school teachers are called to be more than just school professionals. Teaching in a Catholic school is a vocation, a state in life, wherein teachers, by living the gospel message, proclaim that message to their students."

3. Establish and demonstrate healthy psychological boundaries.

". . . teachers are called to love their students and to show this love in the way that they interact with their students. Teachers and students enter a personal relationship, which is characterized by a prudent combination of familiarity and distance and which is adapted to the need of each individual student (Congregation for Catholic Education, 1982, #33). These relationships allow the Catholic school teacher to form with his or her students close bonds that assist in the development of the faith community of the school."[65]

Relationship is fundamental for teacher effectiveness. Effective teachers do not simply teach academic subjects well, they have also established relationships with their students. As the Congregation for Catholic Education (1998) notes:

"Attention is rightly given to the importance of the relations existing among all those who make up the educating community. During

childhood and adolescence a student needs to experience personal relations with outstanding educators, and what is taught has greater influence on the student's formation when placed in a context of personal involvement, genuine reciprocity, coherence of attitudes, lifestyles, and day-to-day behavior."[66]

Providing a context of personal involvement and genuine reciprocity calls for maturity, responsibility, and accountability on the part of the teacher. Teachers, however, must remember that they are adults, not peers, best friends, or social companions to their students. Convey expresses the balance needed by suggesting that the teacher-student relationship should be *"characterized by a prudent combination of familiarity and distance."*[67] This combination should also characterize the relationship of teachers with the parents of their students.

Personal witness, personal relationships, and professional boundaries are the crucial characteristics of Catholic school educators. Ralph Waldo Emerson advised integrity of action.[68] His words have evolved into the contemporary saying: *"What you do speaks so loudly that I cannot hear what you say."*[69]

It is in this sense that student self-discipline is most effectively "caught" and "taught." When teachers demonstrate patterns of self-control, forethought, respectful interaction with others, Gospel values, reverence for God and the things of God, and find ways to redirect frustration or anger, students learn how to translate these aspects of self-discipline into their own lives. They "catch" the meaning of lessons "taught" previously in words. Pondering the challenge of this reality suggests the following questions to Catholic educators:

- What effort do I exert to provide on-going formation for my own soul? Do I participate in days of recollection, retreats, conferences/workshops/in-services for personal enrichment? Do I participate in Mass more often than the Saturday vigil/Sunday liturgies? Do I cultivate the practice of adoration before the Blessed Sacrament? Am I developing the practice of meditating on Sacred Scripture? Am I nourishing a life of prayer?

- Do I give example to students of the behaviors that I ask of them? For example, if I instruct students to cease all activity and give attention to announcements whenever the public address system is operational, do my students observe me at attention or am I tending to teacher projects? When attending Church functions or assemblies, if I expect students to be silent and respectful am I observed giving reverence, attention, and devotion or am I seen talking with another teacher or marking papers?
- Do I demonstrate effort in the kinds of practices that I demand of students, i.e., an organized environment, planning ahead, meeting due dates, respectful demeanor, faithful use of my time, self-control, prudence, etc. If I expect students to be "on task," do I model industry and fidelity, or am I observed engaging in non-class activity or talking with another teacher in the hallway during class time? If I call students to wear their uniform with pride, do I myself dress professionally?

Conditions that Challenge Attitudes of Self-Discipline

The process of helping children to develop Gospel values and habits of responsibility, self-control, respect, and responsiveness requires perseverance, patience, and long-suffering from teachers. The mission becomes exponentially challenging when the conditions of home and society contradict the Gospel. Teachers often experience frustration and resistance. The Congregation for Catholic Schools summarized some of the difficulties that face teacher attempts to evangelize in the third millennium:

> "... new forms of poverty challenge the Catholic school.... those who have lost all sense of meaning in life and lack any type of inspiring ideal, those to whom no values are proposed and who do not know the beauty of faith, who come from families which are broken and incapable of love, often living in situations of material and spiritual poverty, slaves to the new idols of a society, which, not infrequently, promises them only a future of unemployment and marginalization. To these new poor the Catholic school turns in a spirit of love."[70]

Unfortunately, many, if not all, teachers can identify students who suffer some of the wounds of contemporary society. These wounds add to the already difficult task of formation and disrupt classroom life. All children, but especially children such as these, need help in order to hear the voice of God and have the strength to follow it in the midst of their life experiences. Students look to their teachers to be stable, constant, and dependable, and they will put them to the test over and over again. Teachers are called to be a sign of God's love in their students' sometimes chaotic lives. A teacher's "being" can shape their "becoming." H.G. Ginott summarizes the dynamic well:

> *"A teacher never abdicates his moral authority. He does not enter mud-throwing contests with children. His discipline is never bizarre and his correction never sadistic. He lives by the law of compassion, even when challenged by children to defy it. A child often misbehaves in order to elicit reactions that confirm his negative views of adults. He provokes anger and evokes punishment to obtain proof for his convictions. He may be unaware of his evocative powers and feel no responsibility for them. Blindly he goes on creating incidents in which he feels victimized. A teacher can help these children by refusing to dance to their tune, by declining to follow their self-defeating designs. He does not allow children to create his climate or to determine his mood. They cannot constrict his repertory of replies. He withholds predictable responses that reinforce negative expectations. His words are chosen, not triggered; his acts are selected, not compelled."*[71]

Teachers can counter negativity and facilitate growth towards discipleship by incorporating the following seven standards into their teaching styles:

1. Say what you mean and mean what you say.

Keep your word. Follow through on what you say. Do not speak rashly, imprudently, or in anger. Rather, say something like: "I am too disappointed to speak now. I will pray about this situation and we will discuss the matter after lunch." Be succinct. Avoid lengthy lecturing.

2. **No double standards. Be sure that what you say is what you do.**

> You must be an example of any standard for which you hold students responsible. If you call children to perform service projects, share with them a service project that you are performing. If students are required to be at attention in a situation, you, too, must be at attention. If students must stop recess at the bell and go directly to class, so must you. If students are not permitted food or drink during class time, neither are you.

3. **Demonstrate consistency, continuity, and predictability.**

> These words are not synonyms for rigidity or structures that stifle creativity. They mean that, regardless of your mood or preference, whether it is a "good day" or a "not so good day," you maintain your standards with equanimity. Routine, procedure, and system contribute to security and enable students to feel confident about what to expect. If two or more teachers work with the same student or class, coordinate or standardize whatever you can while still honoring your own individuality.

4. **Contain or redirect personal stress, mood, or ego.**

> Do not permit personal hurts or concerns from your private life to infect your professional life. When stress weighs heavy on your heart, ritualize a way of leaving the fear or anxiety at home. For instance, if your spiritual practice includes daily Mass, place your problems on the paten or in the chalice and ask Jesus to take them as grains of wheat and return to you, instead, His body and blood. If you have access to a tabernacle, place your concerns in the tabernacle. Ask Jesus to hold them and heal them and you. Begin the practice of a "prayer dish." A prayer dish is a container with a lid. Create a sacred space in your home or classroom for it. Place your intentions in the dish, thereby

acknowledging you have a problem which needs healing, but which you are unable to fix it on your own. Pray over the people or situations that you put into the dish. Then put the lid on it and go into the day freed from those burdens or worries. If you are wise, you will not "reclaim" the items when you return home. Rather, let the light and fire of the Holy Spirit work on them and on your heart. When you have safe time, talk over the contents with our God. You will be surprised at the outcomes.

5. Use humor to redirect behavior.

Remember the old saying about attracting more flies with honey than with vinegar. A brewing problem can be nipped in the bud with a smile, the twinkle of an eye, an exaggerated question mark on your face as you gaze at the crucifix on the wall, a puzzled-sounding voice speaking aloud to God something like, "How could this be happening?" or "Mitzie is not really trying to push my buttons, is she?" A personal favorite of mine is saying something like, "Allie, I am honored. I heard the rumor that you liked me but I didn't realize that you wanted to spend Saturday with me!" You can count on giggles or laughter after any of those kinds of humor. It breaks the problem and redirects behavior.

6. Save the "big guns" as a last resort.

Keep small things small. Move from the least response towards stronger responses, as needed. Ignore something when you can. The first correction might be merely a raised eyebrow as you continue teaching. Then stand near the student's desk. If more intervention is required, stop speaking while making eye contact with the student. This might be followed by calling on the child directly. If problem behavior still persists, it is time for further action. Whatever you do, a demerit, detention, or timeout should not be the first response. Save those as a last resort.

7. **Demonstrate genuine affection**.

Great hearts are grateful hearts. Express appreciation. Find reasons to say "Thank you." Show regard for students without reference to competence or accomplishment. Find something to share with the student who "bothers" you the most. Perhaps you learn that she likes cats. Every now and then make a cat comment or leave a cat sticker on her desk or tell her about a cat that you saw at the pet store. Be respectful in attitude and speech toward the students. Call them by name, smile, and speak to them the way that you want them to speak to you. Remember that you are the adult. As the adult, initiate contact after an upset. Do not give in to your own hurt feelings. Dismiss or control attitudes of retaliation. Honor confidences. Do not, however, promise confidentiality in matters of abuse, suicide, or psychological issues. Do not tell one student's business to other students or teachers. Avoid discussing students or their families at faculty gatherings. If you are in need of information on a student make an appointment to speak with the professional who can enlighten you, but be clear from the beginning that you are seeking confidential information and that you will keep it confidential. Gossip is a failure of the eighth commandment. Gossip is speaking a person's business, even if it is true, to another person who has no right to the information. Be encouraging. Encouragement is skill-related. It names a skill that the student has already demonstrated, i.e., "I noticed that you read from your library book after you finished your assignments, Scott. That was using your initiative." "I admired the compassion you showed, Ashton, when you anticipated Michael's needs and gave him a tissue." Finally, show that you enjoy the class. Take time for fun. Laugh with the students. Know their interests. Go to a football game or basketball game, stop in on a scout meeting, decorate the room to reflect their interests, etc. Share highlights of your life when you were their age.

Called to be Faithful

At this point, teachers may feel overwhelmed or inadequate. The vocation of Catholic school educators requires effort and virtue far beyond anything involved in preparing coursework. Make no mistake about it. God will supply what is needed. Teachers need only be faithful, willing to try, and willing to start over again and again. Take comfort in the words of Mother Teresa of Calcutta: "*We are not called to be successful, we are called to be faithful.*" After all, one has no power to command success; one has power only over one's own effort and motivation. The result is only God's to control.

Musical artist Steve Green (1988) expresses the call to faithfulness in song. The refrain of *Find Us Faithful,* inspired by the exegesis of 2 Tim. 4: 7-8. St. Paul taught Timothy the same way a master helps to form new teachers. It applies to the vocation of Catholic educators:

> "*Oh may all who come behind us find us faithful*
> May the fire of our devotion light their way
> May the footprints that we leave
> Lead them to believe
> And the lives we live inspire them to obey
> *Oh may all who come behind us find us faithful.*"[72]

To Teachers New to the Profession or Returning to the Profession of Catholic Education:

> " *Let no one look down on you because of your youth, but be a continuing example of love, faith, and purity to believers. . . . Devote yourself to the reading of Scripture, to preaching and teaching. Do not neglect the gift you received . . . Attend to your duties; let them absorb you, so that everyone may see your progress. Watch yourself and watch your teaching. Persevere at both tasks. By doing so you will bring to salvation yourself and all who hear you*" (I Tim. 4: 12-16).

Years ago I heard a keynote speaker address a graduating class of nurses. She told them that in the year following they would, indeed, be the most inexperienced nurses wherever they worked. She suggested that they might have occasion to hear an older nurse criticizing them because they were young and inexperienced. Indeed, the veteran nurse might say something like, *"What does she know? She's just a kid. Why I've been nursing for fifty years."* The keynote speaker told the nurses to examine the criticism carefully. She advised: *"If the nurse was, indeed, nursing for fifty years, then learn everything she has to teach you. But take caution! There is a difference between nursing for fifty years and nursing for one-year times fifty years. You will have very little to learn from the latter."* This story offers food for thought for "young" educators, too. Capitalize on your energy, enthusiasm, and willingness to try new things, delight and excitement at surprising students and being creative. Share those gifts of time and talent; nature and grace with the school community. Be an example to all of openness, possibility, zeal, and spontaneity. Ask for feedback, invite suggestions from veteran teachers, and do a lot of listening and observing. Seek out veteran teachers who make each year unique rather than a carbon copy of years before. Learn all that those teachers have to share.

To Veteran Teachers:

". . . I remind you to stir into flame the gift of God bestowed. . . The Spirit God has given us is no cowardly spirit, but rather one that makes us strong, loving, and wise. Therefore, never be ashamed of your testimony to our Lord. . . but with the strength which comes from God bear your share of the hardship which the gospel entails" (2 Tim. 1: 6-8).

If you entered the new school year as though it was your first class ever, giving thought to planning and preparation, trying new things, exerting effort, energy and enthusiasm, I salute you. You are a master teacher and your school has cause for celebration. If, however, you began this year with the same decorations that were hanging last May, or your decorations are yellowed with age and sun, or your lesson plans are photocopies or printouts of last year's plan, I encourage you to recall your first years of teaching with their inspiration and animating spirit. Recall that nothing was too much trouble, how you enjoyed creating ways to delight the students. Years have a way of jading the spirit. Criticism, misunderstanding, mounting pressures, extended responsibilities, feeling unappreciated, and various other details of the human condition can weigh down a soul. It is easy to slip into monotony and cold detachment, to begin to assume a "we-they" mentality, to exhibit an adversarial attitude. This is not only counterproductive for discipleship; such an atmosphere invites student lethargy and behavioral problems. If school has become more burdensome than invigorating, it is time for a change of grade, a subject change, a different position in the school, a change of schools, or a sabbatical. Sometimes a short break is enough to refresh us, to renew our spirit, and return to us our earlier ideals.

The mission of evangelization requires constant enthusiasm. In the midst of challenges, setbacks, and the stumbling blocks that are inherent in the human condition, we are called to model Christ to our students. We can depend on the presence of the Spirit to instruct our hearts and inspire our steps. Recall that the last words of Jesus in Matthew's gospel: "I am with you always, to the close of the age" (Mt. 28:20). Remember that God does not call the qualified. He qualifies the called!

CHAPTER THREE

The Dynamics
of Discipline

THIS BOOK BEGAN with a look at the gospel notion of discipline which, according to its Latin derivative, means *to grasp or to take instruction.* To Catholic educators, the term means the ability to listen to the voice of another, to understand the message, and to act upon it appropriately and in freedom, without external constraint. We have looked more deeply into the concept of discipline by replacing the terms of external motivation, i.e., control, coercion, punishment, and retaliation with the goals of internal motivation, i.e., inner-direction, responsibility, cooperation, and responsiveness. We considered what elements characterize a culture of discipleship within a school. Finally, we reflected on how the grace of vocation influences the attitudes, approaches, and polices that teachers use to foster self-discipline in students. We were reminded that vocation was indispensable to discipleship and we were invited to incorporate seven standards into our style of interaction with students.

This chapter synthesizes child development theory from a body of scholars: Abidin, Adler, Coopersmith, Dinkmeyer & Dinkmeyer, Dinkmeyer & McKay, Dreikurs, and Erikson.[73] Out of this research has evolved six dynamics of discipline that have affected the understanding of self and the ability to be an effective catalyst for discipleship: (1) effective communication, (2) a balanced style of authority, (3) the connection of needs and behavior, (4) avoidance & redirection of misbehavior, (5) the use of consequences rather than reward or punishment, and (6) the practice of encouragement. This chapter will look at each factor and suggest its implications for discipleship.

EFFECTIVE COMMUNICATION

A visitor to a school can detect the communication climate in a classroom easily. If it is positive and healthy, the environment is characterized by respect, reverence, and openness. Both teacher and students make time for each other and show courtesy in speech and action. Body language demonstrates interest, attentiveness, and recognition of the dignity of the other. During conversation the teacher listens for feelings and honors them, i.e., asking questions that show that he or she is following the conversation. Within the context of a loving communication climate, the hallmarks of effective communication include (1) presence, (2) careful listening, and careful speaking.

Presence

Presence is the gift of connecting emotionally, mentally, and spiritually with another. Presence says: "You are valued. I am aware of you and your needs. I want to interact with you. You are worthy of my time." Presence is demonstrated through attentiveness, eye contact, focus, and emotional connection. Presence recognizes emotional cues, i.e., disappointment, anxiety, or excitement. Consideration of the gift of presence distinguishes four qualities and suggests the following questions to Catholic educators:

Consistency

Human connection is fortified when there is a pattern of speaking and connecting with a person over time, rather than limiting communication to sporadic episodes.
- How often do I make intentional effort to touch base with each of my students?
- Do I make myself available and involved with students at some recess times?

Individualization

Presence suggests that one sees another as an individual, not merely as one member of a class. The larger the class size, the more challenging this becomes. It calls forth creativity on the part of the teacher but it can be accomplished with an endearing nickname, i.e., "my philosopher," or "my dance partner," or a facial or bodily signal, i.e., rolling one's eyes dramatically, brushing one's nose, or a particular sound, e.g., singing or humming the word *Glo-ri-a* from the *refrain* of *Angels We Have Heard on High* when student Gloria passes you in the hallway.

- With how many of my students do I have an individualized connection?
- What can I initiate as an individualized connection for each student on my class list?

Attentiveness

Attentiveness works both ways. Both teacher and student need to demonstrate that they are "clued in" to each other. Certainly, the teacher needs to be alert, aware, and listen respectfully to the student. The student should do the same for the teacher.

- Do I secure the attention of the student before I speak, i.e., establish eye contact and respectful silence that awaits communication?
- Do I wait for student acknowledgement before I continue to speak?
- Do I wait for student response to the question that I ask?
- Do I seek clarification, i.e., "Tell me what you think I said."

History

Long-term presence, i.e., sharing a past full of connecting events, bonds teacher to student. History contributes to relationship, cooperation, and an effective climate for communication. It is an investment that pays high dividends in self-discipline.

- How much do I know of the personal life of my students?
- Do I season my class lessons with acknowledgements, i.e., after Matthew delivers a message and leaves the room, turning to Grace and saying, "Is he still Number One?" or

creating sentences for the weekly spelling test that incorporate student interests.

- Do I repeat positive anecdotes and recall previous connections, i.e., "As I recall, the last time you bet against my team you lived to regret it!"
- Do I know the friendship connections of the students and use those names when dictating the weekly spelling test or when creating math problems, or to illustrate concepts in religion class.

Careful Listening

Careful listening is listening centered in the heart rather than the head. Hearing is the physical act of making sense of different sounds. Listening coordinates the intention of the speaker with the meaning of the words. It is active. It involves verbal and non-verbal skills, as well as care to avoid typical barriers to communication. Careful listening recognizes underlying feelings, motivations, emotional responses, and emotional blocks. The careful listener summarizes what was said and "hears" what was not said. This listener focuses on the student's message and avoid taking over the conversation, lecturing, moralizing, or pontificating. The teacher who is a careful listener nurtures in students the ability to name, claim, and tame their emotions. Listening that is careful fosters personal ownership and responsibility for actions and consequences, cultivates truthfulness, honesty, and integrity, develops discernment and self-discipline, and supports independence. Consideration of the gift of careful listening evokes seven qualities and suggests the following questions to Catholic educators:

Interest Cues

When students attempt to share their thoughts with teachers they look for indications of concern and the intention to participate in the conversation. In their body language teachers should indicate that students are more important than reading, grading papers, filing, etc. This can be accomplished through eye contact, touch, facial expression, and body posture.

- Do I give full attention to a student that eliminates side conversation, looking away toward other centers of focus, or completing tasks during the conversation?

Non-Verbal Affirmations

Recognize that a nod of the head, a smile, a raised eyebrow, or a deep exhaling of breath is non-verbal communication. It says things such as, "I'm with you. I understand what you are saying." "That must have been hard," etc.

- How conscious am I that students need non-verbal affirmation?
- How generous am I with giving affirmation or validating the feelings of my students?

Honor Silence and Tears

When we are comfortable with silence during personal sharing, we honor privacy and allow room for the Spirit to move through the soul of both speaker and the listener. Silence is instructive. Tears, too, often indicate the movement of the Spirit or signs that a core issue is in the process of being revealed. Control the urge to be an instant problem-solver. Look beyond silence and tears and identify the feelings, emotions, blocks, or motivations that have evoked them.

- Do I feel that I have to fill in time with words?
- Am I comfortable with silence?
- Does my style of listening give students "permission" to be touched by the Spirit?

Verbal Encouragement That Does Not Interrupt

A dissonant interruption during conversation breaks the energy and stifles further disclosure. When the momentum is broken, the speaker is often unable to continue. It is usually better to hold questions until the speaker has finished speaking. The use of non-interruptive encouragement illustrates an attentive presence and does not break the speaker's flow. Use words and phrases, such as "humm," "Go on. . .", "That makes sense," "I understand," "Could you say a little more about that?" "Explain that to me again."

- Does my pattern of listening focus on the student's content and encourage disclosure or do I insert my agenda, advice, and direction?

Restating

The ability to restate accurately what another person has said is proof that one has listened with care. After a student has finished speaking, the teacher should summarize in his or her own words what he or she thinks the student has said. For instance, "So what you are saying is . . ." "Now let's see if I understand. . ." "I think that you said. . ."

- Do I practice restating the student's input before responding or giving my opinion?
- Do I listen well or am I planning my rebuttal or problem solving while the student is speaking?

Reflecting

As with the skill of restating, reflecting shows that one has listened well. In reflection statements one demonstrates that one has "heard" feelings and motivations that students have not expressed verbally. Reflective comments may help students to recognize and claim the feelings behind the facts of their stories. For instance, "I sense you have strong feelings about this, perhaps even some fear." "It sounds like you were embarrassed by what Chris said." "Am I hearing that you felt betrayed by the group?" It is not a block to further conversation if one does not interpret the student's statement correctly at the outset. This may help the student to put aside one issue or to state his or her feelings more fully.

- Do I have to be acknowledged as correct in order to feel adequate in conversation with others?
- Can I give students freedom to have their own feelings or do I tend to impose my feelings or opinions on them?

Mirroring

A mirror does not create the image in front of it; it merely reflects what is before it. Mirroring, a quality of careful listening, engages the teacher to reflect back to the student the "bottom line" of what the student is reporting and to ask questions for the purpose of clarification or focus. The teacher serves as facilitator, not judge or jury. Mirroring conversation leads the student to identify his own issue as well as an option or remedy or alternative behavior. During mirroring conversation the teacher checks on student understanding periodically, by saying, i.e., "Tell me what you think I said." "How do you understand what I've said?" "Explain what my words mean to you."

- Do I tend to identify issues for the student, thereby saving time, but removing responsibility from the student?
- Do I facilitate student ownership of issues or behavior by summarizing, questioning and seeking clarification?

Careful listening is a skill that requires practice and patience. Perhaps the deadliest challenge to effective communication occurs when a teacher slips into a problem-solving mode, rather than listening respectfully and limiting verbal comment to affirmation, validation, and reflecting back what was heard. Janet Malone has illustrated nine typical barriers that shut down communication, given in **Table 4**.

TABLE 4
Barriers to Communication[74]

Diagnosing	"What your problem is . . ."
Diverting	"Oh, that's nothing. Wait until I tell what happened to me . . ."
Mind Reading	"Oh, I just knew you were going to say that . . ."
Debating	"I can't believe you see it like that! Obviously, you don't know . . ."
Advising	"What you need to do in this situation. . ."
Criticizing	"You are so dense; I told you that . . ."
Moralizing	"A good Christian would look at it this way . . ."
Patronizing	"Your lack of experience really shows up here. . ."
Being Right	"No, that's not how it is. Let me explain the real facts to you. . ."

- Do I recognize a barrier tendency in my style of communication?
- Does my style of communication help to awaken the soul of the student?

Careful Speaking

Speaking with care implies that information is conveyed clearly and respectfully through word, tone, and gesture. A teacher who speaks carefully addresses students in a respectful tone and by name and does not use negative titles, derogatory nicknames, or impersonal references. Speaking with care implies that what is said is necessary and, if a correction, is conveyed with truth, with respect and with an eye toward instruction and conversion, rather than condemnation or shame. Ginott has captured the essence: *"His [the teacher's] words are chosen, not triggered; his acts are selected, not compelled."*[75]

Effective communication has three aspects: (1) The tone of voice communicates the intention. A sentence can be a request, an option, or a directive. Be sure to modulate your voice to convey the desired intention. (2) Define terms mutually to avoid verbal manipulation or confusion over semantics. Never assume that two people are speaking as one mind merely because the same words are used. (3) Develop the skill of using "I Messages" rather than accusatory language. Rather than making accusations or characterizations of students in unflattering terms, use language that concentrates on the effect(s) that student misbehaviors have on the you. "I Messages" have four parts:

- a "when" phrase in which you state the behavior;
- an "I feel" phrase in which your state your feeling;
- a "because" phrase in which you state the consequences that the behavior has on you; and,
- an "I need/want" phrase that expresses your immediate directive.

Table 5 shows the components of an "I message."

TABLE 5
Components of an "I Message"

When . . .	State the Behavior	**When** music is blaring
I feel . . .	State the Feeling	**I feel** agitated
Because . . . clearly.	State the Consequence	**Because** I cannot think
I want/need . . .	State the Directive	**I need** you to turn the volume down to "three" on the stereo.

DEVELOP A BALANCED STYLE OF AUTHORITY

Authority, the right to rule, sanction, influence, decide, or act for the good of students, is a power vested in teachers. The way a teacher understands authority and the style of practicing authority contributes significantly to the way that children behave both with and away from teachers. When authority is practiced as leadership and responsibility, rather than power and control, discipleship can take root and flourish. Insight into the effect that an authority style has on child response and growth in self-discipline has been reported by Dinkmeyer & McKay, Dreikurs, Nelsen, Popkin, *et al.*[76]

In general, three styles of exercising authority explain much of adult behavior: (1) the giving of orders: an autocratic, authoritarian, controlling type of authority, (2) the *laissez-faire* type of authority, and (3) the giving of choices, i.e., the democratic type of authority. Though all three are used in different circumstances, most teachers tend to adhere to a certain pattern that represents his or her basic philosophy of behavior. One's style tends to come out of one's own experiences in childhood; these experience can dominate or one can shape one's own style. The goal of responsible leadership is to encourage students to exhibit mutual respect, self-control, responsibility, and accountability, personal decision-making, acceptance of consequences, contribution to the common good, the exploration of alternative solutions to obstacles, and the ability to set realistic standards for themselves. Students who regard their teachers as responsible leaders can gain the skills needed to become inner-directed and self-disciplined. Growth in autonomy is thwarted, however, when students see teachers who assume the role of servant, time-keeper, or personal secretary, or when teachers act in ways that are nagging, controlling, over-indulging, over-protecting, domineering, or pitying. *"Though well intentioned,"* reported McCormack, *"such behaviors keep children dependent and rob them of self-confidence, self-control, self-reliance, and the ability to determine personal boundaries and accountability."*[77]

Giving Orders

Teachers who practice the "giving orders" style of authority believe that control must be imposed. Consciously or unconsciously this teacher believes that wisdom resides in her and not in students, merely because she is older and more experienced and, primarily for those reasons, she deserves respect and blind obedience. Of course, "wisdom, age, and grace" (Lk. 2:52) are valued assets but teachers who exercise "giving orders" authority discount the ability of students to be active agents in their own formation. This teacher believes that he or she knows what is good and that student choices must be dictated. This attitude assumes that students, on their own, cannot know what is good. People with such an authoritarian mindset criticize, blame, demand, threaten, nag, and lecture students. They tend to manipulate behavior by the promise of reward or punishment. Controlling teachers assume responsibility for all problems and decisions, set many rules, withdraw privileges, and are tempted to practices of corporal punishment and verbal abuse.

Students respond in various ways to this style of authority. They may exhibit fear, anger, resentment, rebellion, or discouragement. They may overly-conform so as to please or comply only when an adult is present or when a reward is offered. The actions of an autocratic, authoritarian, controlling teacher are often met with retaliation, resistance, or passive-aggressive behavior. The resulting environment is not life-giving and presents an obstacle to the development of discipleship.

Giving In

Teachers who practice the "giving-in" style of authority have a *laissez-faire* policy with respect to student conduct. These teachers feel powerless and overwhelmed and are afraid to take a stand. Whether motivated by wanting to be liked, by being thought of as a "pal," or because the teacher values freedom at the expense of chaos, the *laissez-faire* teacher offers no opinions and makes requests of the students that are easily ignored. When a matter of importance is at stake, the permissive teacher will plead, beg, explain, or try to coax the students into action. Students are generally free to follow their own whims and to make demands of the teacher. On the many occasions that misbehavior surfaces, this teacher will attempt to reason with the students.

Students who experience this style of authority do not receive appropriate guidelines. This is a disservice because children without limits are insecure, inconsistent, and develop behaviors that are socially unacceptable and annoying to others. When this is combined with a tendency to ignore the rights of other students, the result is a child no one likes. Furthermore, the child grows to dislike himself. Children who have a steady diet of doing as they please do not learn to care about others. They do not develop the affective skills that are so essential to human bonding and to conscience-formation, i.e., empathy, sharing, and compassion.

Giving Choices

Teachers who practice the "giving choices" style of authority believe in controlling the situation, not the child. There is a significant difference between the two. This style of responsible leadership is authoritative, not authoritarian. It permits students to take ownership and equal partnership for the classroom enterprise. It encourages independence and decision-making while reserving responsibility for approval of final decisions to the adult.

Teachers who develop this style of leadership practice equality and mutual respect. Whenever appropriate, they involve students in decision-making, giving choices suited to the age and development of the children, while determining necessary limits and boundaries. Within a democratic atmosphere students take ownership for their choices and resulting consequences. Democratic teachers find ways to encourage and validate student initiative. They see their role in education as similar to that of John the Baptist who said of Jesus, *"He must increase, while I must decrease"* (Jn. 3:30). Teachers with this style of authority empower students to take leadership. The teacher moves to the background so that the student can ascend to full potential. This style of leadership prepares students for discipleship.

Students who experience this style of authority become positive, purposeful, enthusiastic, and proud—in the best sense of the word. Thus these students:

> *". . . demonstrate the following characteristics: mutual respect, trust, concern and caring; empathy for others; willingness to listen to others; the ability to focus on strengths rather than weaknesses; commitment to cooperation and participation in conflict resolution; honest sharing of feelings rather than hiding them and bearing resentment; appreciation of common goals with freedom to pursue personal goals; and willingness to accept themselves and others as imperfect and in the process of growth. Behavior problems are minimum in a democratic family [classroom] because true discipline is fostered; discipline that is defined as listening, understanding, integrating, owning, and responding in a life-giving way."*[78]

Each teacher should evaluate their own style of authority and leadership as well as that of their colleagues. Another way to arrive at the answer of authority style is to reflect on the student response to each style. Student response is related to teacher stimulus. Ginott captured the dynamic this way:

> *"I have come to a frightening conclusion.*
> *I am the decisive element in the classroom.*
> *It is my personal approach that creates the climate.*
> *It is my daily mood that makes the weather.*
> *As a teacher I possess tremendous power to make a child's life miserable or joyous.*

I can be a tool of torture or an instrument of inspiration.
I can humiliate or humor, hurt or heal.
In all situations it is my response that decides whether a crisis will be escalated or de-escalated,
And a child humanized or de-humanized."[79]

What a powerful thought! Each educator should take the time to read this material slowly and prayerfully. They should examine the history of their interactions with students, both individually and as a class. If pattern is one of giving choices, this should be continued.; if that of giving in or giving orders, consider the goals of giving choices and prayerfully design an action plan to employ one day at a time. **Table 6** presents a comparison of teacher characteristics and student responses.

TABLE 6
A Comparison of Three Styles of Authority

Giving Orders
(Autocratic, Authoritarian, Controlling)
Belief that control must be imposed

TEACHER CHARACTERISTICS	STUDENT RESPONSES
Criticize, blame, demand, threaten, nag, lecture	Fear, anger, resentment, rebellion, discouragement
Manipulate via reward and punishment	Over-conformist behavior
Take responsibility for problem-solving and decisions	Compliance only when teacher is present
Set many rules	Act in retaliatory ways
Withdraw privileges	Take a stand on issues that the teacher cannot control, i.e., choice of friends
Resort to physical action	

Giving In
(Permissive, Laissez-faire)

Belief in the policy of non-interference in conduct

TEACHER CHARACTERISTICS	STUDENT RESPONSES
Views self as powerless or overwhelmed	Insecurity, inconsistency, lack of self-control
Afraid to take a stand	Socially unacceptable behavior
Offer no opinions, suggestions	Annoying to others
Make requests that are easily ignored	Ignores the rights of others
Plead, beg, explain, coax	Fail to develop affective skills, i.e,. caring about feelings of others, empathy, sharing, compassion. . .

Giving Choices
(Pro-Active, Democratic, Authoritative)

Belief in controlling the situation; not controlling the child

TEACHER CHARACTERISTICS	STUDENT RESPONSES
Practices equality and mutual respect	Shows respect, trust, cooperation, concern, caring
When appropriate, involves students in decision-making	Feels empathy for others
Gives choices suited to age and development	Focuses on strengths rather than weaknesses
Determines necessary limits and boundaries	Accepts self as imperfect and in the process of growth.

CONNECT NEEDS AND BEHAVIOR

All people have four basic needs which are prerequisites for social, spiritual, psychological, and emotional growth:[80] (1) to be loved, i.e., to experience attention, involvement, contribution, and a sense of belonging; (2) to be in control of oneself, i.e., to experience personal power, autonomy, responsibility, and a sense of fruitful independence; (3) to be treated respectfully and reasonably, i.e., justly and fairly, trusted and given consideration and recognition; and, (4) to be competent and relied upon, i.e., to be needed, to accomplish, to be skilled, and capable.

These are the essential elements for the development of positive identity formation, which is fundamental for personal growth, and relationship with others. If left untended, these needs fester into negative, retaliatory, self-defeating, or withdrawing behaviors. When these needs are met they ready one for positive interaction, responsibility, and a sense of connection. Fulfillment of these needs leads a student to become inner-directed, responsible, responsive, and cooperative, the characteristics of a self-disciplined person. Students who do not have these characteristics act out in ways that seek attention or power, seek revenge, or display inadequacy. Dinkmeyer & McKay note that teenagers have three additional needs: excitement, peer acceptance, and superiority.[81] Learning to recognize what motivates student misbehavior is the key to ameliorating the situation in the relationship between teacher and student. The following are suggestions for recognizing the student tendency to misbehavior and appropriate teacher responses. McCormack (1999c) has offered guiding principles to parents aimed at connecting needs to behavior. That advice is repeated here, tailored to the teacher-student relationship.[82]

The goal of misbehavior cannot be determined by the behavior itself. Misbehavior can occur for four reasons: a desire for attention, power, revenge, or to express inadequacy. To identify misbehavior, teachers need to become conscious of and sensitive (1) to their own internal feeling at the time of student misbehavior, (2) to their usual spontaneous-response tendency, and (3) to the way a student tends to react to teacher attempts at correction. This process is not as easy as it reads! It takes time to develop this level of sensitivity and sometimes children are motivated by more than one need. But the teacher who learns to name her *predominant* internal response, i.e., annoyance, anger, hurt, or powerlessness, and to control her automatic knee-jerk reaction to the misbehavior is able to address the major cause of the student's pain and the healing process can then begin. Consider the situation of a student who instigates a commotion in the back of the classroom and interrupts you while you are working with a small group of students an the side of the classroom.

1. If the student's goal is ATTENTION, your spontaneous internal reaction is to feel annoyed and bothered. In your mind you think, "Oh, you are such a pest!" or "Now what?" You want to remind her or coax her not to interrupt and if you do respond to the behavior, she stops temporarily.

2. If the student's goal is POWER, you feel provoked and angry and sense that your authority is threatened. You feel like gritting your teeth and saying something like, "Who do you think you are?" or "You don't know your place. Who died and left you boss?" You have a tendency to scold or to give in. If you challenge her, she intensifies her action because she wants to win.

3. If the student's goal is REVENGE, you feel deeply hurt by her interruption and lack of self-control. You think, "How could she do this to me after all I've done for her?" You have a tendency to retaliate and get even with her, to teach her a lesson! For some reason, the student wants to get even and to punish you and when she senses that you are hurt, she continues hurtful behavior.

4. If the student's goal is related to INADEQUACY, you feel despair and hopelessness. You feel like saying, "I give up. I don't know what more I can do. I've tried everything I know to help her. This is hopeless." Your feeling identifies what the student already feels and concludes about herself. She has already given up on herself. She feels inadequate and unable to anything right. Your reaction demonstrates that you agree with her that nothing can be done. She then becomes passive and shows no improvement.

At this point in our discussion of needs and behavior, a pastoral caution is well advised! Be gentle with yourself as you strive to develop the level of sensitivity required to redirect misbehavior towards conversion. Intellectual grasp of the concepts and process is not a guarantee of successful implementation. St. Paul voiced it well: *"What happens is that I do, not the good I will to do, but the evil* [life-blocking responses/reactions] *I do not intend"* (Rom. 7: 19).

Through these behaviors, students are sending messages that they perceive themselves to be need-deprived and that they are attempting to feed this void by seeking attention, power, revenge, or a feeling of competence or adequacy. Teachers make a difference in the formation of students when they feed these hungers in positive ways and respond proactively. Strategies to apply for each style of misbehavior are suggested in **Table 7**, along with a summary of what has been said about identifying (1) fundamental needs, (2) mistaken beliefs of students, (3) the goals of misbehavior, (4) a teacher's internal feeling at the time of student misbehavior, (5) the usual teacher response-tendency, and, (6) the way a student tends to react when the teacher makes a correction.

TABLE 7
Understanding the Dynamic of Misbehavior

Identity Element #1: Security	
Fundamental Need	To be loved (attention, involvement, contribution, belonging)
Motivating Belief	*I belong when I am noticed or being served by the Teacher.*
Goal of Student Misbehavior	Attention
Teacher Internal Feeling	Feel annoyed, bothered, pestered
Usual Teacher Response-Tendency	Remind, coax
Student Reaction to Correction	Misbehavior stops temporarily
Strategies:	
When possible, ignore misbehavior.	Catch student being good.
At neutral times give attention for positive behavior	Teach student valid ways to ask for attention; to identify needs
Avoid undue "service", baby-ing, smothering	Stand close by; give eye contact, touch
Give clear explanations, boundaries, limits	Determine a secret signal (an emotional connection)
Schedule time with the student on a regular basis	Ask a direct question of the student
Say what you mean and mean what you say.	Practice what you preach.
PRO-ACTIVE REMEDY:	Teacher practices that foster SECURITY

Identity Element #2: Autonomy

Fundamental Need	To be in control of self(power, autonomy, responsibility, independence)
Motivating Belief	*I belong if I am in control or proving that no one else can control me.*
Goal of Student Misbehavior	Power
Teacher Internal Feeling	Feel provoked, angry, threatened
Usual Teacher Response-Tendency	Fight back or give in
Student Reaction to Correction	Misbehavior intensifies
Strategies:	
Withdraw from conflict.	Allow the student to have voice and choice.
Act kindly but firmly, without speaking.	Grant legitimate power.
Redirect the focus to a constructive action.	Involve the student in decision-making.
At neutral times ask for help and give responsibilities.	Delegate responsibility.
Do not fight or give in.	Emphasize effort more than result.
PRO-ACTIVE REMEDY:	Teacher practices that foster AUTONOMY

Identity Element #3: Initiative

Fundamental Need	To be treated respectfully, justly, and fairly(trusted, treated reasonably, given consideration, recognition, validation)
Motivating Belief	*When I am hurt I need to hurt others.*
Goal of Student Misbehavior	Revenge
Teacher Internal Feeling	Feel hurt
Usual Teacher Response-Tendency	Retaliate, get even with the student
Student Reaction to Correction	Student senses that she has been successful in hurting the teacher and she continues to act in hurtful ways.
Strategies:	
Avoid feeling hurt.	Build a caring relationship.

Withdraw from the cycle of revenge.	Focus on the effect that choices have on relationships.
Show respect and depend upon the student.	Teach appropriate expressions of feelings.
Speak sentences of encouragement.	Foster the dignity of the student.
Separate the behavior from the student.	Celebrate ideas and process more than product.
PRO-ACTIVE REMEDY:	Teacher practices that foster INITIATIVE

Identity Element #4: Industry

Fundamental Need	To be competent, relied upon, needed(accomplishment, capability, skilled)
Motivating Belief	*I belong by convincing others not to expect anything from me. I am unable and useless.*
Goal of Student Misbehavior	To have an excuse for failure and inadequacy
Teacher Internal Feeling	Despair, hopelessness, "what's the use?" "I give up"
Usual Teacher Response-Tendency	Frustration, passive response, no response
Student Reaction to Correction	Student becomes passive; shows no improvement
Strategies:	
Stop all criticism.	Eliminate situations of competition until inner strength develops.
Arrange for small successes.	Modify instructional methods.
Focus on assets.	Encourage positive self-talk.
Avoid pity and despair.	Reframe "I can't" statements.
Provide skill training.	Suggest the use of the word "yet".
Work side-by-side through a challenging task.	Teach ways to become *unstuck* from negativity.
Plan your work; work your plan.	Foster organizational skills.
PRO-ACTIVE REMEDY:	Teacher practices that foster INDUSTRY

Teachers who attend to their own reactions when students misbehave become skilled at identifying the causes of student misbehavior. They also develop (1) effective responses, (2) ways to re-direct the student, and, (3) proactive strategies to pre-empt misbehavior. For example, recognizing the purpose behind student behavior enables the instructor to decide whether the student is in need of belonging, involvement, or contribution. Ignore the misbehavior if possible; if the behavior must be addressed, do so as simply and quietly as possible. At another point, involve the student in positive activity and catch him being good, helpful, etc. Simple cries for attention may be settled merely by standing close to the student or giving him eye contact. Ask the student a question while appearing to unaffected by the annoying behavior. If the student demonstrates attention-needs as a pattern, schedule time with the student in ways that communicate a sense of belonging. Teach the student valid ways to ask for attention, determine a secret signal that can serve to connect you with the student emotionally. Teach the student how to name his need. Affirm that belonging, contribution, involvement, cooperation, and giving, as well as receiving, attention are the basic needs of all people. Communicate to the student that he or she deserves attention, but that there are more appropriate ways to feed this need. The proactive remedy for attention-seeking is to provide regular, consistent practices that foster security. Such practices will be discussed later in this chapter.

When the desire for power motivates student behavior you will know it. The teacher will be provoked and tempted to retaliate. Power struggles arise when legitimate experiences of power, autonomy, responsibility, or independence are denied. The teacher who recognizes a power struggle for what it is does not exacerbate the conflict or engage in a battle of wits. Rather, she acts kindly and calmly, but stays her course. Her actions speak for her; she does not need to argue or be drawn into a battle. Simple power behaviors can be redirected by focusing the student on constructive activity and fed at neutral times by asking help from the student, delegating responsibilities, providing a pattern of granting voice and choice, vesting the student with legitimate power, and involving him in decision-making. The pro-active remedy for power-seeking involves practices of autonomy.

Students are hurt if they think they have been slighted, treated unjustly or unreasonably, or disrespected. Their hurt translates into vengeful behavior. What they really need is to experience trust, i.e., given consideration, recognition, and validation for their persons and their ideas. It is natural for the teacher to feel hurt by student behavior. A teacher who understands how to read the motivation behind the misbehavior will withdraw from the cycle of revenge. He will try to work against his hurt feelings, remembering that the student is a child and the teacher is an adult. During neutral times, appropriate responses to this kind of misbehavior include: depending on the student, demonstrating respect, speaking words of encouragement, building a caring relationship, and fostering the dignity of the student. During occasions of correction, avoid making character judgements of the student. Instead, focus on the behavior and the effect that choices have on relational living. Teach the student appropriate expressions for his feelings and concentrate on ideas and process more than end results. Certainly results and products matter but if we focus on the elements that we can control, i.e., effort, ideas, and details of process, they will yield positive results. Avoid vengeful behavior by incorporating teacher practices that foster initiative.

Feelings of inferiority are deadly. They lead students to experience despair and hopelessness, and to develop an attitude of "What's the use? I give up." Teachers may tend to feel frustration and inadequacy, to assume a passive position, or to become hardened to the plight of the student. The student who feels inferior, however, is like the lost sheep of the gospel (Jn.10). Teachers are called to shepherd the student toward competence and accomplishment. Teachers who recognize signs of student feelings of inferiority, inadequacy, uselessness, or passivity relieve this stress by replacing criticism with encouragement and eliminating situations of competition. A student with an underdeveloped sense of industry predicts failure at the outset of most situations and expects to be inferior in any competition with other students. They benefit more from the self-competition expressed in a popular saying: "Good, better, best, never let it rest until your good is better and your better is your best". When feelings of inferiority are replaced by confidence, then competition may even be motivational. Teachers build student-competence when they arrange for small successes, focus on the student's assets, provide skill training and practice, work side-by side in challenging tasks, and modify instructional methods. Teachers help to lift students from feelings of inferiority when they: (1) encourage positive self-talk, i.e., "I conquered fractions last year. In time I will improve in geometry," or, "Rome wasn't built in a day. I just need to do one step at a time," or "I may be weak in math, but I am strong in conversational skills." Teachers also (2) reframe "I can't" statements with the use of "yet," e.g., "I can't outline a paragraph," becomes " I do not understand how to outline yet, but I can pick out the topic sentence," or "I can't play basketball yet, but I can improve with practice." They (3) demonstrate ways to get out of negativity. Students who feel inferior hardly know where to begin to change their patterns. Organizational skills are an essential start, i.e., arranging books and materials in the desk and school bag, copying assignments, streamlining folders and portfolios, breaking a block of time into smaller increments, maintaining a calendar, building structure into every event, and learning how to set goals, define reasonable objectives, and determine checkpoints to keep on track. Industry is the best remedy for avoiding feelings of inferiority. Teachers who help students to learn how to plan their work and work their plan contribute to the development of industry.

There are three sources that are particularly helpful when trying to identify student needs, related behavior, and appropriate teacher responses. Though addressed to parents, the literature of the STEP program (Systematic Training for Effective Parenting), provides valuable insight to teachers. STEP explains the concepts of needs and behavior in divisions of age: birth through age five, ages six through twelve, and teen years.[83] DeBruyn & Larson (1984) describe in detail 117 student behaviors and misbehaviors in terms of needs, the primary causes of student misbehavior, helpful teacher strategies, and common mistakes teachers make when dealing with the student.[84] *The MASTER Teacher* has made that work available as a free teacher resource online at www.disciplinehelp.com.

AVOID AND REDIRECT MISBEHAVIOR

It is crucial for teachers to assume a proactive stance to feed these hungers. Every child needs to be loved, to be in control, to be treated respectfully, justly, and fairly, and to be competent and relied upon by his teacher and peers. A student who experiences herself as connected, responsible, respected, and capable usually makes life-giving, self-disciplined choices because the goal of her behavior is to maintain and strengthen her already-developing positive identity. A student who feels denied a basic need takes action to have that need met, to protect herself, or to retaliate for her pain. The elements of positive identity formation serve as proactive practices that help students to avoid misbehavior in the first place. Proactive security practices counteract the student need for attention. Practices of autonomy deflect the need for power struggles. Practices of initiative avert revenge-based behavior. The pain of inadequacy or despair is obviated by the habit of industry. When security, autonomy, initiative, and industry are characteristic of a teacher's leadership style, misbehavior occurs rarely and, if incidents of misbehavior do surface, students are redirected to life-giving choices through the application of the needed practice. The connection between the proactive elements of positive identity formation and the needs/behavior/misbehavior of students is recorded in Table 7. To be skilled in applying proactive practices, teachers need an understanding of the elements of identity formation.[85]

This chapter presents: (1) an overview of the five elements that are crucial to positive identity, and, (2) it names characteristic behaviors that support the growth of each element. McCormack has offered parents an summary explanation of the elements and their characteristics. The advice applies to teachers as well:

"These five elements are the simple essentials of soul formation. Love of God, neighbor, and self depends upon their development. The elements

name WHAT is necessary; and the description cites the kinds of practices that foster growth of the element but they do not define HOW to provide the experience. The HOW is personal. Each parent [teacher] brings personal experience, philosophy, abilities, limitations, woundedness, awareness and, spirituality to child-rearing [student formation]. There are varied ways to accomplish the task of identity formation and self-esteem foundation. The HOW can vary; the WHAT is the constant factor in the development of identity. Parents [teachers] have the potential to provide this substantial formation."[86]

Security

Security is the sense of stability, trust, and confidence that comes from experiencing a pattern of predictable responses from significant people in our lives. If one's experience is that of repeated disappointment, abandonment, or frustration, mistrust and insecurity results. When security is characteristic of a person, DRIVE develops as a basic life strength and HOPE flowers as a characteristic life virtue. A student who has a sense of security is generally self-confident, believes that he can depend on others, feels safe, is trusting, and has an inner confidence that all things will work satisfactorily. The insecure child is often fearful, frustrated, or uncertain. She doubts the sincerity of others and is suspicious. She approaches new people, situations, and tasks with a feeling of apprehension. Children who have a pervasive feeling of insecurity, convey an aimless, lost attitude. Teachers need to intervene in the lives of such children. McCormack (2001b) reported that *"Security formation occurs by integrating on a consistent basis the components that create a pattern of reliability."*[87] These components include:

- **Routine, Procedure, System.** When daily functions of schooling can be reduced to "automatic control," energy is available for the unpredictable events of the day. This enables the student to deal successfully with stress, with more readiness to hear God's voice. Routine, procedure, and system serve that purpose. For example, is there a pattern of expectation for opening and ending class, receiving absentee assignments, checking/submitting homework, getting to and from the library, etc.?

- **Safety—physical and emotional.** Emotional and physical safety reinforces inner security. While issues of physical safety are generally dealt with, those of emotional security need more consideration. Do students know that disrespect, name-calling, mean jokes, put downs, and bullying are not tolerated in the classroom? Is privacy safeguarded, are confidences kept? Can students identify and handle emotions constructively? What emotional boundaries are established within the teacher as well as for students?

- **Consistency, Continuity, Predictability.** Consistent expectations, limits, responses, and consequences require decisions based on non-emotional reasoning and applied consistently. When policy shifts from day-to-day or mood to mood, students develop insecurity because they are not able to predict and plan accordingly. It is vital that teachers form the habit of saying only what they mean and acting on what they say. Do not make false promises or threats and do not speak in anger. It is better to say you are too angry to talk about an incident, to set a discussion time for later, and calm down before that discussion. If, however, you create a pattern of not following through with announced consequences, you lose credibility and the student is denied a valuable experience of formation.

All students benefit from a teacher who establishes routines, procedures, safety precautions, and a system for the ordinary, predictable activities that comprise school life. If a teacher is perceived as consistent and predictable, students will become more confident and have energy available to take on the challenges of growing. Continuity establishes the kinds of boundaries and limits that promote trust. Teachers who show consistently that their word can be trusted contribute vitally to the development of a sense of security within students. There are many ways to inculcate security. McCormack has arranged ideas from a body of educators into sixty themes. Those common to all age levels of students included adult supervision, attentive presence, classroom organization, class work strategies, communication, discipline, encouragement, individualization, interdependence, participation, routine procedures, safety, and student-centered classroom ownership.[88]

Autonomy

Autonomy is a deliberate, free-will decision to perform self-initiated acts. It is respectful independence, inner authority, responsibility, and self-reliance that permits a student to make appropriate decisions and manage many of the details of daily living without the need of supervision. If, however, self-initiated efforts repeatedly meet with failure or disapproval, a child learns self-doubt, to second guess himself, and he feels humiliated. When autonomy is characteristic of a person, SELF-CONTROL develops as a basic life strength and WILLPOWER flowers as a characteristic life virtue. A student who is developing a sense of autonomy does not require external motivation in order to make positive choices. He practices self-control and is nurtured by the experience of personal power that self-governing produces. He is able to assume the freedom to initiate without being told what to do. He learns to represent himself in a positive way that respects the rights of others. He learns to be assertive without being aggressive. The student who lacks autonomy, on the other hand, lacks a balanced sense of personal limit and capabilities and does not know how far he or she should go in a situation. He is afraid of testing personal limits for fear of failure. It is not unusual that he begins to look to others to make decisions for him. Generally afraid of making a mistake, this student would rather do nothing than err. A non-autonomous child is painfully self-conscious and wants to be invisible, fading into the background. He feels that he cannot be accepted, and often has a sense of regret, easily feels disapproval or censure from others, and, actually, expects disapproval. Often he will turn anger against himself or against others. It is not surprising then that some of these children become schoolyard bullies, walking containers of resentment and anger. Teachers can help to change this by consistent application of teacher practices that foster autonomy. McCormack says that: "*Autonomy formation occurs by integrating on a consistent basis the components that create a pattern of self reliance.*"[89] These components include:

- **Responsible Independence.** All children need to experience themselves as independent, powerful, and in control. The personal satisfaction that accompanies self-control becomes self-motivating and develops into leadership. Age-appropriate responsibilities that receive acknowledgement and appreciation lead to increased autonomy. Expect responsible independence and do nothing for students that they are capable of doing for themselves. Ask for volunteers. Appoint subject captains. Provide options. Facilitate student ownership for planning and executing events.

- **Self-Governance**: Acknowledging one's behavior and accepting the consequences of one's choices leads to the development of integrity and self-governance. Lessen the fear of mistakes. Transform mistakes into stepping stones for growth. Respond, rather than react, to misbehavior. Speak calmly and respectfully and involve the student in identifying the issue clearly, applying natural or logical consequences. Follow up with a "business as usual" attitude.

- **Respectful Assertiveness.** Teach students appropriate ways express their needs, agreements, and disagreements with other students with role-playing, role-reversal, and discussion of examples that arise on TV, video, in literature, or observable situations. Reflect the wisdom contained in the saying, "*We can learn something from everyone, even if it is what not to do!*"

- **Accountability.** Emphasize effort more than results. In the midst of failure or disappointment, guide students to identify the aspects of their decision that illustrate effort, i.e., time management, organizational skills, advance planning, and formatting, etc. Lead students to acknowledge responsibility for their decisions and behaviors, both positive and negative.

Any practice that fosters self-reliance, independence, and personal maturity contributes to the development of autonomy. When teachers provide tools such as geoboards/math manipulatives, computers, or puzzles for use when class assignments are finished before class deadline, they are supporting independence. They encourage self-governance and accountability when they institute a coupon system that permits students to leave the room to use the lavatory or to get a drink of water, or expect students to monitor sports equipment check-out, organize lunch orders, or direct dismissal procedures. Teachers encourage autonomous, self-reliant behavior when they publicly acknowledge a student who has demonstrated responsible independence, or when they establish a work system like the Workshop Way, developed by Sr. Grace Pilon (www.workshopway.com), or when they design a contract with choices for participation. Autonomy is fostered by any practice that defines boundaries, establishes criteria, builds accountability, fosters independence, and empowers students to assume responsibility for themselves and ownership for the community. McCormack (1999d) organizes examples of teacher and administrative practices that support the development of student autonomy into forty-eight themes. Those common to all age levels of students included affirmation, attentive presence, cooperative or interdependent learning, creative expression, emotional safety, encouragement, homework, personal responsibility, respectful assertiveness, structured independence, and student-centered classroom management.[90]

Initiative

Initiative is an inner sense of self-motivation that comes from repeated experiences of initiating plans and conquering tasks without being told to do so. A student with initiative becomes a self-starter, is able to assume personal responsibility, accepts the challenge of new tasks and is not paralyzed by mistakes. On the other hand, a child with a sense of guilt hesitates to try new things and is paralyzed by the fear of making mistakes. When initiative is more characteristic than guilt, DIRECTION becomes a basic life strength and PURPOSE evolves as a basic life virtue. Initiative fuels a sense of vision that gives birth to goals and personal ownership for the future. It is a natural deterrent to restlessness and passive-aggressive behavior. Initiative enables a student to aim high, to develop the ability to analyze what is needed to complete a project, and to take pleasure in assembling the pieces into a finished product. When a student has her own ideas of what to do and how to do it and those ideas are acknowledged as appropriate and accepted as "good enough," initiative develops. If, however, her ideas are replaced by the preference of teacher or her peers, or pre-established plans are substituted, she learns to second-guess herself, to feel guilty, and to become passive. If teachers give the impression that mistakes are unforgivable, the student is hesitant to try new things and expects to fail before the task is even attempted. Teachers can recognize students who are more defined by guilt than initiative. They are quick to apologize for happenings or circumstances for which they are not really responsible. Often they show a sense of resignation or they are settle for less than what they want or deserve. Students who lack initiative require repeated suggestions and monitoring from others to start a project or task. They prefer clear, specific, detailed, and directed instructions and these instructions often need to be repeated. What can a teacher do to move students toward initiative rather than frustration and guilt? McCormack reports that *"Initiative formation occurs by integrating on a consistent basis the components that create a pattern of self motivation."*[91] These components include:

- **Exposure to Varied Experiences.** Use varied experiences to help students define their interests, develop skills, identify capabilities, and define personal limits. Travel, videos/ CDs, TV programs, books, observation of others, and vicarious situations of real life or literature, followed by discussion, have the potential to spark initiative.

- **Emphasize Ideas and Process Over Product.** Often the success of a product is contingent on factors beyond one's control. Concentration only on the end product can encourage a defeatist attitude. A more constructive approach is to measure success by the ideas generated and processes followed. Acknowledge ideas for creativity, ingenuity, usefulness, timeliness, or forethought and encourage the elements of process, i.e., planning, organization, time management, teamwork, and distribution of labor. These are skills that will be needed throughout life.

- **Model Recovery after Mistakes.** Show that mistakes are redeemable when we learn from them, that mistakes are temporary setbacks, not permanent obstacles. Help students to view mistakes as a way to learn new approaches, methods, skills, or visions to apply to a future assignment or situation.

- **Prepare Material, Tools and Other Resources Related to Success.** Equip students with the tools needed for the successful completion of a task. Students are responsible for their own writing instruments, paper, etc., but teachers are responsible for inculcating the skills related to a project. For instance, before assigning a term paper, the teacher has first to teach how to use library resources, how to outline, how to organize notes, how to summarize information without plagiarizing, how to cite sources, how to make footnotes, how to create a bibliography, etc.

- **Freedom Tempered with Responsibility.** Freedom is the essential criterion for growth in initiative. Students need the freedom to be risk-takers, to make mistakes, and to bear the consequences of their choices with responsibility for restitution. Responsibility without freedom is slavery and it breeds resentment and revenge. Freedom without responsibility is license and it breeds selfishness and havoc. Unless physically or morally harmful, permit the student to experience the consequences of her choices. Avoid an "I told you so" attitude. Let experience be the best teacher.

- **Standards and Deadlines.** Establish standards, rubrics (criteria that describe levels of performance or understanding for a particular topic), and due dates that are reasonable and realistic. When you ask too much of a student you frustrate him; when you ask too little you insult him. Once you have determined a deadline that is reasonable and realistic, stick to it.

Teachers can encourage initiative in many ways. For example, giving an assignment on Monday that is due Thursday allows the student to manage his or her own time and resources; this balances freedom with responsibility and consequences. Class meetings balance personal needs with the common good and teach the art of negotiation and responsible freedom. Initiative is fostered when a teacher uses student ideas or provides opportunities for extra credit projects in which students pursue topics of their own choosing. Teachers invite academic freedom and give to students unspoken permission to pursue their own thoughts when they use various strategies to demonstrate understanding of a concept, show students that different processes can be used to arrive at one goal or conclusion (i.e., storyboard, student-written examinations, etc.). All students benefit from a teacher who applies knowledge of personality typology, learning-style preference, and multiple intelligence research to lesson planning as well as to experiences of prayer and who encourages student resourcefulness, personal responsibility, varied activities, repeated exercise in choosing, a pattern of valuing the elements of a process, and application of lessons learned from constructive criticism. Teachers help to stretch student experiences when they provide learning stations, contracts, challenge activities, career days, clubs, extracurricular projects, literature, film, or music that widens the student's horizons. These are only a few examples of ways that teachers can contribute to student growth in initiative.[92] McCormack has reported multiple examples of teacher and administrative practices that support the development of student initiative within grade levels and across age interests. These ideas were grouped the ideas into thirty-nine themes. Those common to all age levels of students included accentuating the positive, celebrating individuality, developing leadership, using developmental assignments or assignments completed over time, encouraging interdependence and personal responsibility, providing positive reinforcement, preparing for success, establishing opportunities for structured independence, and facilitating student-centered classroom management.

Industry

Industry is the capacity to be persistent, diligent, to complete a task, and to create a systematic approach for problem solving and fulfilling responsibilities. The consequence of industry is the interior perception of competence. Industry develops within the student METHOD as a basic life strength and COMPETENCE as a basic life virtue. The opposite of industry is inferiority. We all know what disasters follow when a student believes himself to be inferior. Teachers must work tirelessly to help students develop the behaviors that facilitate growth in industry. The industrious student sticks to projects, hobbies, or tasks, and completes them in a timely manner without reminders. He perseveres, is productive, and enjoys the satisfaction of accomplishment. He gives consistent attention to projects over time and works with order and system. His organizational style need not duplicate the teacher's. It is uniquely his and it works for him. The opposite is true of the student who lacks industry. If he repeatedly experiences himself as unfinished or inadequate, he learns to settle for less and to view himself as mediocre or defeated before he begins, developing an inner sense of inferiority. He fails to recognize ability or giftedness within himself and begins to believe that he is of little importance compared to others. He may become painfully timid, fearful, and shy or show exaggerated aggressiveness to compensate for his feelings of inferiority. What can a teacher do to stem the tide of inferiority and influence attitudes of accomplishment? McCormack[93] has suggested that the components of industry include:

- **Steady Care Over Time.** Choreograph activities and assignments that force the student to work on a task on an on-going basis, i.e., a service project, a book report completed in several segments, a contract project that engages the student once a week for a month, etc. Steady care over time, whether convenient or inconvenient, builds endurance and teaches the reality that good things take time.

- **Productivity.** "Success begets success." The satisfaction of completing a task will become self-motivating. Document past challenges that became success stories through perseverance, i.e., portfolios, special notebooks or copybooks, performance folders on display, classroom or hallway decorations, class publishing center, etc.

- **Follow-Through.** Expect accountability: students must finish what they begin, they must meet due dates, and accept the consequences, whether positive or negative. If a task is viewed as threatening or overwhelming, work side by side with students as a coach or demonstrator.

- **Time Management and Long Range Projects.** Use a calendar or chore charts to divide long-range projects into smaller goals and deadlines. Check for accountability in a timely manner. When project pieces pile up, the task can seem overwhelming and this can paralyze the student. This frustration becomes life-blocking.

- **"Plan Your Work and Work Your Plan."** Emphasize the maxim, *"If you fail to plan, you plan to fail."* Provide steady practice in planning: (1) set a goal, (2) identify the objectives that need to be operational in order to achieve the goal, (3) name specific behaviors to meet the objective, (4) establish a manageable timeline and system for completion, and (5) decide how to monitor accountability. Apply goal setting skills regularly, i.e., planning special lunchtime activities for a holiday, deciding how to raise money for the missions, preparing for a special art project, or how to honor the Blessed Mother during May.

Teachers model industry by performing their own tasks in a timely manner and by organizing the classroom for efficiency. Using a classroom calendar to post upcoming events, e.g., tests, projects, assignments, socials, and student-sponsored activities, is an effective way to teach long-range planning, to communicate deadlines, and to enable students to use foresight to work in advance of deadlines. Cooperative learning groups can also help students to organize and monitor their time. Teachers need to teach the membership functions within a cooperative learning group. Developing a sense of industry is the major function of elementary schools everywhere. It is the focal time in psychological growth, between ages six and twelve to set the foundation. Industry development requires a steady diet of productivity, accomplishment, sticking to a task, getting a job done on repeated occasions, having a sense of being able to move on the next step or phase of a project, being diligent, and developing a personal systematic approach to tasks and responsibilities. Be creative and persistent in orchestrating opportunities to develop industry. Teachers and administrators from several schools have offered suggestions for teacher practices that support the development of student industry within grade level and across age interests. McCormack has arranged these ideas into thirty themes. Those common to all age levels included the attentive presence of the teacher, class work strategies that highlight productivity and a history of accomplishment, encouragement, participation, public recognition of steady effort, establishment and enforcement of realistic standards in work, and instruction to students on time management.[94]

- **Genuine Affection.** This is cultivated when a student experiences appreciation, acceptance, and perceives that he or she is valued, apart from competence or accomplishment. When unconditional acceptance is present, openness, and respect for others develop as life strengths in the student. Unconditional love is the experience of being cherished, preferred, sought, esteemed, appreciated, accepted, and valued by a significant person when you have done nothing to "earn" it. This was the experience of Zaccheus (Lk. 19:1-10), the apostles (Mt. 4:18-22), Levi (Mk. 2: 13-14), the adulterous woman (Jn. 8: 3-11), and the crucified criminal (Lk. 23:39-43), to name a few people who knew themselves to be sinners, perceived themselves as unworthy, and experienced the unconditional acceptance, respect, and welcome of Jesus. Indeed, at those times when a student seems to be going out of her way to be her worst self, unconditional love is an experience of mercy! It is in the practice of genuine affection that the teacher most closely resembles God and is most likely to bring a child closer to accepting the love that God has for them. Yancey (1977) has reduced the meaning of unconditional love to three sentences:

"There is nothing we do can make God love us more.
There is nothing we do can make God love us less.
God already loves us as much as an infinite God can possibly love."[95]

Repeated recognition as a person who is unique, respected, and enjoyed is fundamental to formation. Children do not want to be compared to others, either individually or as a class. They want to be appreciated for who they are. They need to experience fairness, justice, respect, trust, reasonableness, consideration, and recognition as individuals in order to feel loved. Children want to know that you like them, that you can spend time with them just having fun, and to have you laugh, joke, and tease in loving ways. McCormack[96] suggests characteristic components of genuine affection which include:

- **Acceptance.** Acceptance of a person and approval of behavior are separate issues. As Nelson (1987) reminds us: *"Children need to know they are more important than anything they do."*[97] Dinkmeyer and McKay (1996) offer this advice: "The first step in establishing a healthy atmosphere is to accept the child. This does not mean condoning all behavior. It is possible to disapprove of certain conduct without rejecting the child as a person. Tone of voice and manner must imply that the person is valued, even though the present act is not. It is essential to separate the deed from the doer. Consequences, for example, must be applied in the spirit of friendliness."[98] Acceptance is welcoming and hospitable, showing respect, care, and affection. Acceptance regards a person as satisfactory aside from her behavior. The fine line that exists between acceptance and approval needs to be expressed carefully. For example, when correction is necessary, separate the behavior from her person, saying something like, *"Sally, your sense of humor is a gift and one of the things that I enjoy about you, but your remarks to Alex were hurtful. Restitution is required. Let me know how you decide to handle it."*

- **Valued Preference, Individualization and Inclusion.** These are interrelated components of unconditional love. Students seek reassurance that they have particular significance to their teacher. They want the teacher to relate to them individually, responding to the particular circumstances of their personality and needs, while at the same time they are measuring fairness and equality within the class. It is a two-edged sword. On one hand, they want independent treatment; on the other hand, they want to be one among equals in the class. A teacher, therefore, should be generous in the practice of the virtues of affection. Beyond that, anticipate and acknowledge student radar when you can, i.e., *"Tony, last week you picked our lunchtime book. Today, Shawn, you can choose the video."* Be creative and proactive about inclusivity: choose students from a class list, draw a name from a deck of cards, name sticks, or student call cards, etc.

- **Appreciation.** Great hearts are grateful hearts. Appreciation readies the heart for relationship because it is an expression of admiration and recognition of effort. We need to know that we are not taken for granted and that effort on our part makes a difference to others.

- **Validation and Affirmation.** Look beyond results! Validation means that you view the student's thoughts, conclusions, decision, or feelings as sound, i.e., satisfactory, substantial, or reliable. Affirmation is a positive statement of achievement, suggesting that the outcome fulfills the goal.

- **Respectful Attitude and Speech.** Self-respect is the fruit of appreciation, validation, and affirmation. It is enhanced when teachers demonstrate respect for the student in attitude and speech, i.e., addressing the student by name and making eye contact vs. barking orders; thoughtful listening and questioning vs. interrupting or preaching; body language that is welcoming vs. body language that is dismissive; and, using given names or loving nicknames vs. derogatory or put-down titles.

- **Teacher-initiated Contact and Forgiveness.** The adult has is obliged to "break the ice" after an incident. Regardless of the hurt inflicted by the student, a teacher must instruct through example, showing how to work through discomfort, to express responsibility, to apologize to ask forgiveness, to receive forgiveness, and to let go of the sting. Forgiveness is proactive. It acknowledges that wrong has been done, but it pardons the offense and the offender. Pardon means that anger and resentment are replaced with grace and second chances.

- **Confidentiality.** Children are sensitive to the opinions of others. They are embarrassed and ashamed to hear their faults described. Keep their private matters confidential, especially their failures. Whenever possible make corrections in private.

- **Encouragement.** Eliminate criticism and be generous with encouragement. Encouragement is skill-directed and focuses on the assets, efforts, and strengths of the student, i.e., "You showed compassion and initiative when you included Chris in the game," or "You were angry but you used words instead of hitting. I am glad that you remembered."

Providing recognition and communicating genuine affection for students, each of whom has a unique personality and way of perceiving things, can appear to be an unattainable goal. The question of how to do that was asked of fifty-two teachers from five elementary schools who contributed to the research reported by McCormack. Her research revealed that:

"Teachers of many grades communicate affection by greeting each student in the morning with conversation, eye contact, touch, and a smile. Most of them acknowledge or celebrate student birthdays and accomplishments; many write an affirming note on an unexpected occasion. Some teachers use nonverbal communication such as a smile, a thumbs-up, or a quick nod of approval." [99]

Repetitions of responses occurred across grade lines. With respect to this chapter, it is sufficient merely to provide eighteen themes around which the specific suggestions were grouped: give students affirmation: be genuine; begin anew; recognize behavior and increase motivation; recognize birthdays; schedule de-stress time; offer encouragement; exercise fairness and equality; remember that humor helps; focus on individualization; promote independence; encourage interdependence (team spirit; cooperative learning); engage in one-on-one interaction; communicate with school parents; offer positive feedback frequently; establish a respectful and nurturing classroom environment; set up a superstar spotlight; practice teacher outreach and (teacher-initiated communication).

Students from a variety of middle-school settings were asked a related question: "What advice would you offer teachers so that they can help students to develop positive self-esteem?" Student responses seem to parallel the suggestions that teachers gave for establishing genuine affection. The student responses fell into six categories: (1) demonstrate respect for students; (2) balance respect with friendliness rather than fear; (3) win student cooperation and performance through affirmation; (4) teach students how to learn from mistakes, (5) reach out to students who have hard times; and (6) help to build unity and friendship in the class.[100]

USE CONSEQUENCES RATHER THAN REWARD OR PUNISHMENT

Not only are punishments and rewards ineffective methods of imparting discipline, they are actually obstacles to discipleship because both methods are rooted in external motivation and both are controlled by the teacher rather than the student. Consequences, either natural or logical, are effective alternatives since they are instructive, respectful, and give control to the child. *"Consequences,"* McCormack has suggested, *"hold children responsible for their choices, allow them to develop and own a personal code of behavior, and permit them to learn from experiences that are impersonal, i.e., hunger, tiredness, tardiness. Consequences teach the reality of the social order which is impersonally related to their choices, behaviors, and misbehaviors."*[101]

Punishment, on the other hand, is a penalty inflicted for an offense. It encourages further misbehavior because it is usually perceived by the student as unfair, arbitrary, hurtful, unreasonable, or disproportionate to the offense. Punishment is often characterized by threats, yelling, put-downs, taking things away, spanking, and hitting. Rewards, like punishment, are also intended to control or manipulate behavior. Though they are attractive and produce quick results, rewards disrespect the student by denying him the formation opportunities to develop autonomy, initiative, and industry which are vital to self-discipline. Rewards make the teacher responsible for student behavior, not the student. Rewards encourage the student to conclude that appropriate behavior is required only when a teacher is present. Rewards foster an attitude of "What's in it for me" and "Does it count?" Barbara Coloroso remarked that children "who are consistently bribed and rewarded are likely to grow into adults who are overly dependent on others for approval and recognition, lacking their own self-confidence and sense of responsibility."[102]

It is important to note that what has been said about rewards does not obviate the value of periodic celebrating student or class effort at internalizing and demonstrating values related to school success. Many teachers, for example, create a ritual to commemorate student progress in completing homework carefully (diligence) every day during a week (consistency) or celebrating class effort at a specific skill, e.g., being ready for closing prayers (anticipation-planning) without a reminder (autonomy, responsible independence). Celebrations vary from personal "credit cards" that document effort and eventually are exchanged for a chance ticket to be used in a monthly drawing of prizes to class participation in an extra fifteen minutes of "DEAR time" (Drop Everything and Read). Some people would suggest that there seems to be a fine line of difference between rewards and celebrations. Though both involve cause and effect, I would suggest that celebrations differ from rewards in four significant ways: (1) Rewards are motivated by the desire to force student behavior to comply with teacher preferences. Celebrations validate freely chosen student behaviors that earn recognition based on pre-advertised criteria. (2) The focus of celebration shifts from mere outward observance (accomplishing tasks) to internal strengths (developing lifelong values). (3) The values, i.e., time management, self-control, responsible independence, are defined as the cause of festivity. (4) Rewards are immediate stimulus-response payoffs while celebrations are intermittent and sometimes spontaneous. Consider "Celebration" a synonym for positive consequence in that the criteria is reasonable, it is known in advance, and it respects the dignity of the student to chose. Celebrations may be particularly useful to introduce young children to self-discipline when they are in the stage of concrete thinking. As B. Bettelheim (1987) reflected:

> " [a child] cannot learn self-control before he is mature enough to
> understand why it is a necessary and advantageous ability to acquire.
> . . . Only after we have reached the age at which we are able to make

our own decisions can we learn to be self-controlled; this can be fairly early, but not before we can reason on our own, since self-control is based on the wish to act on the basis of one's own decisions, arrived at through one's own deliberations."[103]

Consequences can be either natural or logical. Natural consequences are outcomes that occur without teacher intervention. For example, a student who chooses not to wear a coat on an icy day will get cold. A student who fails to submit an assignment on due date will be subject to whatever policy has been established. Natural consequences should be allowed to run their course unless they are (1) dangerous, (2) interfere with the rights of others, or (3) the child does not realize the harmful impact that her choices have on others. At such times, logical consequences need to be applied. Logical consequences are outcomes that require the intervention of another person. For example, if a student is uncooperative during small group work, the teacher can tell the student to abide by the discussion rules and stay with the group or lose the privilege of group activity and accomplish the assignment independently. A matter-of-fact tone of voice, friendly attitude, good will, and willingness to accept the student's decision are essential characteristics in formulating consequences.

Effective logical consequences are predetermined and public, not arbitrary solutions to an immediate problem. Forethought is vital to logical consequences, as are four other characteristics: (1) The consequence is *related* to the behavior, i.e., the outcome is congruent with the offense. (2) The consequence is *respectful* of persons, i.e., the choice respects the needs of both teacher and student; it is conveyed with a sense of abandon to whatever choice the student makes, and it separates the action from the person. (3) The consequence is *reasonable*, i.e., the consequence is fair, balanced, impartial, and concerned with the present moment. (4) The consequence must be *enforced*, i.e., the pre-determined consequence actually occurs. Dinkmeyer and McKay suggest twelve principles to guide parents in the use of natural and logical consequences. Their advice applies to teachers as well:

- Understand the child's goals, behavior and emotions.

- Be both firm and kind.
- Don't try to be a "good" parent [teacher]. (Do not overprotect or take on the   responsibilities of the child [student].
- Become more consistent in your actions.
- Separate the deed from the doer.
- Encourage independence.
- Avoid pity.
- Do not become over-concerned about what other people think.
- Recognize who owns the problem.
- Talk less, act more.
- Refuse to fight or to give in.
- Let all the children share responsibility.[104]

Be cautious! The difference between punishment and logical consequences is not always obvious. No matter how logical the action may seem, if the teacher's tone is judgmental or harsh, the attitude overbearing or bullying, or the demands absolute, the teacher's actions will be punitive and demeaning. They will consist of punishment, not the kind of consequence that leads to self-discipline. R.L. Curwin and A.N. Mendler provide an example of each and then explain the distinction:

> *Example of Consequence: "You are responsible to get any missed information or make up any work missed while you are late."*
>
> *Example of Punishment: "Miss entire class sitting in the principal's office, then make up the work."*
>
> *"The main differences between consequences and punishments in the above examples are that the consequences are simple, direct, related to the rule, logical (that is, they are natural outcomes of the rule violation), and instructive. Punishments are not related to the rule, are not natural extensions of the rule, and tend to generate anxiety, hostility, and resentment in the student. Natural and logical consequences help teach proper behavior. Effective consequences are also direct and simple."[105]*

PRACTICE ENCOURAGEMENT

Encouragement is a process of focusing on the assets and strengths of a student. It promotes self-confidence, inner courage, and self-esteem because it gives verbal recognition and validation of a student's specific, skill-related accomplishment or character development. For example, "It was thoughtful of you to include David in the game. You showed leadership," spoken to the student who showed initiative, compassion and courage in the face of peer pressure to invite an unpopular student to join in play, provided validation of that student's virtue. The statement "You demonstrated initiative when you anticipated the need for dictionaries and passed them out to the class," recognizes the student for organizational skills and for being a self-starter. Encouraging statements motivate a child and help him to believe in himself and his ability; they show him how to find his own strengths and special qualities. Encouragement provides direction in self-discipline by identifying a specific behavior that the student can choose to duplicate in the future.

Praise is an expression of approval, but it does not identify the specific reason for the affirmation, i.e., "That's terrific!" or "I admire you." Without telling the student why her action was terrific or in what way you admire her, the student remains unclear about how to replicate your respect. Although well-meaning, praise is a type of reward. It "feels" arbitrary and serves as a social control. Over-reliance on praise leads a student to conclude that her worth depends upon the opinion of others. The danger there is that when we care primarily about what others think, we allow others to measure our behavior and choices, rather than internalizing our own code of values. McCormack identifies ways in which this dynamic is counterproductive to the development of self-discipline:

> "The child directs his efforts at receiving the praise rather than at internalizing a life-giving value. Often he will stop cooperating when praise is not received. Some children become addicted to praise, and others become resentful and revel because they feel like puppets who no longer want to live according to the expectations of others."[106]

Praise feels great at the moment it is given but when the moment passes the student does not know what the words meant. It is not instructive for him. "Carlos, thank you for being patient at the Hot Lunch check out counter" is far more instructive and validating than "You're a good boy, Carlos." Though many persons think of praise and encouragement as synonyms, they can be contrasted in several vital ways. A study of the contrasts is provided in **Table 8**.

TABLE 8
A Contrast between Encouragement and Praise

ENCOURAGEMENT	PRAISE
An expression of specific, skill-related assets and strengths that were demonstrated by a student	An expression of approval that does not identify the specific reason for the affirmation.
Carlos, thank you for being patient at the Hot Lunch check out counter.	*You're a good boy, Carlos!"*
Concerned with effort	Concerned with results.
Unearned; a gift	Earned; a reward
Communicates awareness of effort and feelings	Communicates judgment and expectation
Fosters self-evaluation	Relies on the evaluation of others
Focuses on the deed (action)	Focuses on the person (worth)
Demonstrates empathy	Concerned with conformity
Inspires independence	Inspires dependence
Is respectful	Is patronizing
Notices improvement	Looks at results
Asks open-ended questions that involve the student in self-evaluation of skills	Uses "should" statements

Nelson (1987) advises that "the successful use of encouragement requires (1) adult attitudes of respect, (2) interest in the child's point of view, and, (3) a desire to influence skills that will lead the child to self-confident independence" (p. 103). She suggested four questions to keep in mind when deciding whether the statements you make to children are praise statements or encouragement statements:

1. Am I inspiriting self-evaluation or dependence on the evaluation of others?
2. Am I being respectful or patronizing?
3. Am I seeing the child's point of view or only my own?
4. Would I make this comment to a friend?

Encouragement is the language of love because you express acceptance, enjoyment, appreciation, faith in the student, and awareness of improvement in effort. Encouragement fosters student reflection and self-evaluation, both of which are essential elements for discipleship. Think about the ways that you could express validation of the students in your class. Examples of the language of encouragement are suggested in **Table 9.**

TABLE 9
Examples of the Language of Encouragement

Acceptance	You seem to like that activity.
Confidence	Knowing you, I am sure you will do fine. I have confidence in your judgment.That's a rough one, but you conquered outlining last month. I think you'll conquer this skill, too.
Appreciation	Thanks, I really appreciate (specific) because it makes my job easier.You have an eye for detail. That drawing is really intricate.
Contribution	The Shamrock group needs your help on (specific).
Assets	You have experience in (specific). Would you do that for the class?
Effort	It looks as if you spent a lot of time thinking that through.
Improvement	You may not feel that you've reached your goal, but look how far you've come! (Be specific.)
Self-Evaluation	How do you feel about your work? With what part of the project are you most satisfied? What is your special contribution to team spirit?

A PRAYERFUL REFLECTION FOR TEACHER CONSCIOUSNESS-RAISING

It is the hope of the author that consideration of the material of this chapter will provide teachers with validation of their efforts, clarification of their objectives, and guide them to adapt the dynamics of discipline, i.e., effective communication, balanced authority style, awareness of human needs and causes of misbehavior, use of consequences and practice of encouragement in order to best serve the formational needs of their students. In this chapter, teachers were invited to take personal inventory of their styles of communication and authority, to understand and know how to connect basic student needs with misbehavior, to anticipate and provide formation with practices of security, autonomy, initiative, industry, and genuine affection, to review or explore ways to avoid and redirect misbehavior, to practice the use of consequences and eliminate the mentality of reward and punishment, and, to replace non-communication, negativity, or praise with statements of encouragement. Is it any wonder that teachers often feel stretched beyond their limits?

One educator considered these tasks. Sister Carol Nagel, IHM, of Holy Innocents School (Philadelphia, PA) was moved to prayer when she heard the song, *"May I Be His Love"* (Troccoli, 1995). She correlated lyrics from this song with the dynamics of discipline and her connection concluded with a prayerful examination of the teacher-student relationship. Nagel calls her work *"Turning Prayer into Action."*[107] In this prayer of imagination she speaks with students. She extracted the "prayer words" of the song, line by line, (they appear here in italics). For each prayer-thought she posed questions for her teacher-soul.

Sometimes I can say all the wrong words.
- Can I allow my speech to reflect The Word at all costs, and to say what is best for you to hear, not just what I want to say?
- Can I speak words of encouragement that are life-giving and uplifting?

Sometimes I can think of only me.
- Can I put myself aside in favor or your security and safety?
- Can I consider more how <u>you</u> feel than how I feel?
- May I model self-direction and self-confidence instead of self-promotion so that you learn autonomy?

I know that my pride can hide the tenderness . . .
- Can gentleness replace harshness in my words and actions toward you?
- Can I give you the right to be right and respect your choices?

. . . that longs to show I care.
- Can I be free and frequent in saying THANK YOU, for after all, you teach me every day?
- Can you have confidence that I accept, appreciate and value you for <u>who</u> you are?

May I be His love for you.
- Can I model productivity and competence so that you will develop industry?
- Can I separate the <u>action</u> from the <u>person</u> so that you learn justice, not judgmentalism?

May I lift your eyes toward heaven.
- Can I not so much rule as guide; not so much control as lead?
- Can my peacefulness soothe your anger and guide you to solutions?

May I come to you and lead you to His light.
- Can partnership and cooperation be the norm rather than power struggles?
- May I model the profitable use of choices and their consequences as the road to wisdom?

Refrain:
May I cry His tears for you.
- Can I be your comfort when you are hurting and cushion your falls with compassion?

- Can I teach you that mistakes are a part of life, but if used constructively, they can be master teachers?
- Can I stand by you when accountability is difficult?

May I be the place that you can run to . . .
- Can I use honest encouragement as a catalyst for self-motivation?
- Can my standards and expectation be reasonable and achievable so that you meet with success?
- Can I teach you respectful assertiveness rather than passivity?

. . . where you'll hear His voice . . .
- Can I listen with my heart as well as my ears and respond rather than react to what you have to say?
- Can my words to you, no matter what your words to me, speak kindness, understanding and fairness?
- Can I handle situations such that I honor and validate your feelings?
- Can I listen reflectively when you . . .

. . . and see Him in my eyes.
- May we together look for and build on your talents.
- May I help you transform your weakness into strengths.

All your life, may I be His love.
- Can I teach you that the <u>person</u> is always lovable, although behavior may not be acceptable?
- May wholeness and happiness be the product of our relationship.
- Can I <u>plan</u> for your growth in Christ-centered values?

Verse 2:
I want to live my life for His glory . . .
- Can Jesus' great Act of Redemption be the model for teaching you that every*one* and every*thing* can be redeemed?
- Can I live the words of John the Baptist, "He must increase and I must decrease"?

. . . and to hold His word here in my heart.
- Can I look to Scripture as the source of my life's direction so that your life will take on meaning?

. . . to let His Spirit fill every part of me . . .
- Can I teach you, and then expect resourcefulness rather than dependence?
- May my striving for holiness be evident to you, and may your growth in holiness be daily a priority for me.

. . . so I'll leave Him everywhere.
- May I teach you to recognize, defend and live gospel values.
- May you and every child who encounters me realize that you are meeting Jesus.

And I know . . .
- Can I believe in you and in my own sacred trust as teacher (parent)?
- Can I depend on you to see a task through and not give up?

. . . that only when I follow Him. . .
- May God's will be my guide and directing forces so that I will see it in every situation.

. . . can I begin to love.
- May every learning of a simple concept or a complex life lesson be an exercise in the positive.
- Can I allow you to take responsibility within your abilities so that you can learn independence?

Refrain Repeats: "May I cry His tears for you . . . All your life, may I be His love."

I pray I'll be His Love.
May His love make me what He has called me to be!
Amen!

CHAPTER FOUR

Structure for Success

SPORTS ENTHUSIASTS AGREE that the best defense is a good offense. Benjamin Franklin put it differently: "*An ounce of prevention is worth a pound of cure.*" No matter how it is expressed, many problems can be averted by forethought. When a teacher thinks ahead about predictable glitches, makes preparation, establishes routine, and structures the classroom environment for success, that teacher is exercising proactive leadership. Routine, procedure, and system not only foster growth in student security, they create a culture of self-discipline.

Some teachers as well as students express a "survival mentality." We all appreciate our holidays, we all look forward to vacation time, and in geographical regions that experience snow we keep alive the hope that a snow holiday will be declared. Those teachers, however, who have a "survive mentality" begin in earnest, early in the school year, to count the days to the next holiday. Theirs is a spirit of drudgery, doom and gloom, rather than enthusiasm for the present moment. School for them has become a task, rather than a vocation. Since they are not exercising the skill of creative forethought, school becomes a torture to be endured rather than an opportunity to be explored. Some personalities are just overwhelmed by the multi-tasking required. They lose focus and become paralyzed rather than organized. It is the purpose of this chapter to review some teacher tips that may serve to replace "survive" with "thrive." This topic is open-ended and not exhaustive in scope or depth. There is no limit to the kinds of teacher practices that can produce effective results in terms of effort, energy, and enthusiasm in a classroom. Furthermore, a variety of classroom management books, i.e., Nelson, Duffy, Escobar, Ortolano, & Owen-Sohocki (2001); Nelson, Lott, & Glenn (2000); Watson (1998); Wong & Wong (1998) are available at any major bookstore or through instructional programs (MASTER Teacher, 1991, 1995, 2002), or via the informative and highly entertaining video series of Harry Wong (1996). This chapter, therefore, is limited in scope to six topics for consideration and discussion:

(1) Housekeeping;
(2) Daily Routine;
(3) Class Period Procedure;
(4) Student Grouping/Group Work;
(5) Monitoring/Reporting Self-Discipline; and,
(6) Homework.

It is the author's hope that the content of this chapter will become a springboard for discussion among colleagues and a vehicle for idea exchange among faculty members. It is the experience of the author that when teachers structure for success they create an atmosphere of respect, cooperation, and joy-filled learning, which, in turn,, fosters self-discipline and makes teaching an adventurous enterprise.

HOUSEKEEPING

- **Curriculum Pacing.** Before the school year begins, create a skeleton calendar of each week and month of the school year for each subject taught, perhaps five squares across and ten squares down. Eliminate or show abbreviated weeks for conventional interruptions to the curriculum, i.e. standardized testing, report card conferences,: faculty meetings and teacher inservice days, holidays, Christmas play practices, etc. The result will be a more realistic calendar. With curriculum guidelines, state standards, expectations, and textbooks nearby, indicate in the blocks the work you hope to cover. From the skeleton calendar write your weekly lesson plan. Of course, there will be deviations from the ideal of the skeleton calendar, but it will serve to keep you on course. Often a teacher who by-passes the overview planning comes to the end of the year with unfinished business. That is unacceptable because it creates an atmosphere of mediocrity. In the absence of challenge, students tend to become restlessness and some settle for inferior effort and accomplishment.

- **Lesson Planning.** Schools, dioceses, and districts may have specific requirements for lesson planning to which a teacher must adhere. Follow the expectations of your teacher contract and handbook. Good lesson plans keep students challenged and on task. Plan books are legal documents. Write legibly or type. Label subjects and time schedule. A stranger should be able to discern from the lesson plan book exactly what to do. Clearly state:
  (1) a measurable, attainable aim/purpose, i.e., compute the perimeter of rectangles through measuring and formula;
  (2) content/sources of the work, i.e., text p.125, teacher worksheet of figures, student notebooks, chalkboard, overhead/transparencies, student rulers;
  (3) procedures, i.e., maintenance sheet column 3, flash card drill, illustrate measuring via transparency; measure the perimeter of three given rectangles, elicit rule (P=2l + 2w), apply the rule at board and in notebooks, practice even # 1-12;
  (4) evaluation, i.e., observation, participation, self-correction of notebook work; and, (5) homework, i.e., contract #3, 4, 5 due Friday.

- Holidays, such as the day before Christmas, deserve special mention. Children will probably be in a "party mentality." Plan the day. It does not need to be as elaborate as the usual plan, but something like this is helpful: prayer, a half-hour organized class lesson/activity of holiday theme, a holiday handout, i.e., crossword puzzle, acrostic, poem contest, art project; exchange of gifts and cards, recess; video/CD or story telling, party (ugh!), cleanup, pack up, dimmed lights and soft music with a reading of the Christmas Scriptures, etc. The bottom line is to control the situation before the situation controls you!

- **Record Keeping.** Maintain accurate records of tests, quizzes, homework assignments, and any other graded work. Devise a system for dating and labeling each entry. It should be easy for you to see a grade and know what the assignment was, when it was assigned, and what the due date or test date was. Return papers in a timely manner.

- **Bulletin Boards and Classroom Décor.** The classroom is "home" to students. Make it attractive, warm, and inviting. Let the classroom appearance send a message to students about the caliber of presentation that should inform their own work. Make decorations instructive and coordinate posters, etc. with the curriculum. Involve students in decorating the room, especially the religious bulletin board. Maintain chalkboards or whiteboards so that they, too, look professional. Reserve chalkboards for teaching and student writing. Do not cover boards with posters, etc. Before the school year begins, many teachers "line" their chalkboards using a black wide felt tip marker and yardstick. The lining is visible for the year and it guides handwriting and positioning of numerals during math classes. Devise a method for classroom cleaning and organization so that students take pride in the appearance of the room. Little details contribute to an atmosphere of excellence. Publish or display student work. The classroom is a workroom with projects in process. It is appropriate to display work in various stages of completion. A word of caution, however, is offered regarding the hallway or places of public display. Student work that appears in public needs to be well done or have corrections showing, indicating the standard of performance for which the school is striving.

- **Student Call Cards.** Some teachers use call cards to ensure that all students have equal opportunity to participate orally in the class. An index card can serve the same purpose. One card per student, bearing the name and, perhaps, the preferred nickname of the student. Some teachers create subject columns on the cards and use them to indicate participation. The cards can be shuffled each day. Call cards are effective in maintaining student alertness during a lesson but some students can feel threatened because they are "put on the spot" in front of their peers. Consequently I recommend that students be free to say "pass" if they are not prepared to respond when their name is called. If you find a student "passing" too often, private discussion and follow up is advised.

- **Seating Chart.** However seating is determined, maintain an up-to-date chart. It serves many uses, i.e., attendance taking in silence, coding for behavior, documenting participation, or making teacher substitution more manageable.

- **Signal for Attention.** Determine a respectful and efficient way to gain student attention when noise levels rise or when student groups are diligently at work, but class attention is required. Avoid ringing a bell, raising your voice, pouting, or displaying displeasure. H.K. Wong suggests a technique which has helped many teachers.[108] On the first day of school explain that there will be times that you need attention when the class is otherwise occupied. Tell the class that whenever the need arises, no matter where they are or what they are doing, you will raise your hand and you will stop speaking. Anyone who sees you is to raise his/her hand and stop speaking. Anyone who sees any student with a raised hand is to raise his/her own hand and stop speaking. Then practice it a few times. Get the students involved in conversation with others and, in the midst of it, raise your hand. Once all understand the signal, let the rest of the year flow on.

- **Smile Awhile.** Do yourself a favor! Let your face muscles relax completely and then look at yourself in the mirror. Is that relaxed face one that appears happy, welcoming, energetic, interested in others or compassionate? Or, does it convey anger, boredom, or annoyance? Students read a teacher's face all day long. If you discover that your face, when in neutral, might be construed as "Our teacher is mad at us," or "My teacher doesn't like me," then be purposeful about smiling. Become conscious of your face and body language. Communicate through both that you are happy in your vocation and that you like your work and your class.

- **Substitute Teacher.** Teacher attendance is vital. As much as possible schedule personal business for after-school hours, weekends, and vacation time. In the event that you do need to have a substitute teacher, be prepared! Write lesson plans that promote continuity in student learning. Leave an up-to-date seating chart, a time schedule, a report of typical procedures, several copies of the class list, the names of students who have special charges, and any special needs that must be tended to. In other words, prepare whatever will make the day move smoothly with the least disruption to the students and their learning. Create a Substitute Emergency Kit with everything needed to move "survive" into "thrive." If the emergency plan includes a duplicated paper, have a set run off and in the box. If the plan calls for a video, CD, or some form of equipment, leave express instructions about how the substitute can locate the needed items. Prepare students for what you expect of them in the event that you are ever absent from class.

- **Student Desks & Possessions.** Show students how to fit textbooks and supplies into their desks. If there are additional places where students store books or materials demonstrate order there. Organize shelves, lockers, and coat rooms, etc. Regularly take time for clean up and restore order if it has disappeared. If you use homework folders or test folders, teach organizational skills pertaining to them and help students to organize their school lives. It is insufficient to say, "By now he should know how to keep a desk." If the student needs help to organize, give the help. Teach students how to cover books and be responsible for book stewardship. Help students to see that their external expressions often are indicators of their internal reality. If student desks are too small to accommodate all of their texts, collect some and shelve them elsewhere. It is helpful if students are assigned a student number. Stack books in piles of 1-5, 6-10, etc., with the numbers showing on the spine of the book covers. Each time the books are needed, one student from each of the groups can distribute and collect them. Methods can be established to share the responsibility. One teacher for instance, created a mini-flip chart of five sheets of cardboard, one sheet for each day of the week. The sheets were held together by a ring, on a hook in front of the classroom. Monday had the numbers 1, 6, 11, 16, 21. Tuesday was numbered 2, 7, 12, 17, 22. Wednesday: 3, 8, 13, 18, 23 and so on. The numbers indicated which students were in charge of books on each of the days of the week. Those numbers evolved into other uses also.

- **Student Notebooks & Papers.** Establish the procedure of writing the date, the objective, and the source of content on the chalkboard for each lesson you teach. Instruct students that their notebooks must record the same information, e.g., 10-22-04 – Addition of Fractions, p. 58. Show students the proper format for heading a paper. One school designed a common heading and then produced a large poster facsimile about 28"x36," posted in every classroom and lab.

- **Classroom Procedures.** Practice procedures for turning in papers, collecting or redistributing materials, collecting coats and personal belongings, where to find assignments given during absence, where to find copies of papers that were distributed, etc. Many teachers create an absentee form on 8.5 x 11" paper. It might say: "Welcome Back. We missed you, ___" with a designation for each subject and the subtitles, "class work" and "homework." The class secretary adds to the sheet as the school day goes on, collecting any handouts that were given to the class. At the end of the day the entire packet is stapled together and stored in a teacher-designated spot. When the absentee student returns, re-entry is smooth and adaptations to the assignments can be made easily and individually tailored.

- **Mechanics of Written Work.** All teachers, regardless of curriculum assignment, are language teachers. The science teacher and the social studies teacher also give attention to use of pencil or ink, cross outs, spelling, punctuation, erasures, etc. Hold students accountable for grade level expectations and support that effort in every written effort of the student.

- **Classroom Charges.** Share responsibility for the cooperative running of the school year. Arrange for classroom charges and provide for rotation so that all students serve in some way regularly. Be fair in rotating the high priority jobs.

DAILY ROUTINE

- **Classroom & Class Readiness.** Before leaving for the day, set up for the next school day. Make sure that paper duplication is done, materials are ready, opening messages, etc., are printed on the chalkboard. If you use the custom of a thought for the day or a journal sentence starter, or if there is an anticipated schedule change, write it on the board before you leave. Unless the teacher handbook stipulates otherwise, arrive at least fifteen minutes before the morning bell. Prepare the room for temperature and ventilation, and organize yourself for the day. Once the children arrive, you need to be attentive to them and class needs, not your own business.

- **Prayers.** Establish a prayer routine for the beginning of each school day, before and after lunch, and at dismissal. Students enjoy taking turns as prayer leaders. Whether you are a departmental teacher, PE teacher, or science or computer lab teacher, begin the class period with prayer. Schedule time so that the prayer is respectful.

- **Morning Arrival & Departmental Switch.** At the beginning of the school day and/or class, set the tone by way of a routine that focuses, centers, and calms the students. For instance, soft music upon arrival, a focus question on the chalkboard about which the students can think and write three sentences in their notebook, or the homework assignment book open on the desk so that teacher can check for parent signatures while students are writing. Set a timer to limit the opening activities. While students are thus engaged, take attendance with the use of a seating chart and distribute special notices, etc. When the timer sounds, begin the class prayer and move immediately into your lesson plan.

- **Lunch Time Procedure.** Take time in the beginning of the year (and more often if necessary) to practice lunch time procedures. i.e., travelling and seating arrangements, care of the table, return of chairs, use of sports equipment, check out system, proper use of lavatories, etc.

- **Dismissal Procedure.** Make this time calm, deliberate, and purposeful. Be on time. Do not keep students, other teachers, car pools, or parents waiting. Teach students how to care for their space, their belongings, and the overall care of the classroom. When students leave for home, the classroom should be left in orderly condition. If lines are involved in dismissal, take time to practice the procedures involved.

- **Holidays** like Thanksgiving, Christmas, Easter, and the last day of school deserve special mention. Clean up and pack up in advance of dismissal time. When all is in readiness, read a story to the class or involve them in a prayer experience or an activity that allows them to remain in their seats. When the dismissal bell rings both you and the students will have a gracious beginning to the holiday.

CLASS PERIOD PROCEDURE – Because no two days are the same and teachers are called to adapt to changing circumstances all too often, there probably is no class period procedure that is foolproof and always applicable. With that in mind, the following guideline is for the "ideal" day. A 40-45 minute class period should include:

- Transition time [2 minutes]: a song, poem, recorded music or recitation that occurs while students are arriving at their desks or exchanging books from one subject to the next;
- Class Prayer [2 minutes];
- Homework Check [no more than 5 minutes] or collect homework;
- Review Previous Work [5 minutes]: flash cards, oral summaries, quiz, maintenance question sheet, oral check of homework, Tic-Tac-Toe, See 'n Touch vocabulary words, Seven-Up, etc.;
- Present the Lesson [10 minutes]: *present* , i.e., with eye contact and enthusiasm, explain, demonstrate, ask leading questions, etc. without reading from the book or having students read the text aloud not teacher-read or student-read;
- Student Application [10-15 minutes]: Students work with the material that was presented while teacher supervises and interacts with students as necessary;
- Summarize the lesson [3 minutes]; possibly assign homework;

GROUP WORK – Generally, children enjoy group activities and cooperative learning. They particularly like the break from independent activity. However, it takes skill to ensure that groups are focused and on task. If grades are involved in the group endeavor, tensions enter into the dynamic, since many students would rather work alone than be disadvantaged by the group.

Self-grouping by students, on the other hand, can result in hurt feelings of those called last or left out. This is a topic that deserves consideration among colleagues. To begin that conversation, consider the following remarks about techniques, rubrics, and grading as a beginning.

Techniques of Grouping

Certainly there is merit in letting students pick a group with which to experience learning but there is also need to learn to work in a group with those not of one's choosing. Furthermore, it protects the feelings of all students since no one is left out or chosen last. A teacher can always pre-determine groups and post a listing. This allows for placement of personalities and abilities. Limit the number to four or five students. Be sensitive to individual needs, though. It may be pastoral to permit a student who wishes to work alone to do so. Beyond that, I offer three suggestions for time-efficient, on-the-spot grouping.

- **Clock Appointments.** Introduce this process as a "getting to know you" activity. Give the students a worksheet with a large clock on it and twelve interest questions with space for written responses. Create questions such as, "How many people live in your house right now?" or "Name your three favorite colors," or "Name your favorite movie from this year or last year," etc. The questions should be age-appropriate. Without explaining the purpose of the clock, instruct the students to write their answers to the twelve questions. Then, taking only question number one, have the students circulate among each other to find ONE student who has an answer that matches theirs. If the question response was a number, like 6, let the student accept a range of +1 and −1. In other words, the student whose answer was 6 can accept a 5, 6, or 7 as a matching response. When two students match each other, they exchange papers and write their autograph next to the ONE on the clock. Each student may sign with only one student. If students remain unmatched, pair them up and instruct them to exchange autographs. Once the pairs are settled, the autographed student is eliminated from being a partner on future questions. Now repeat the pattern for question number two. After it is settled, go on to number three, etc. Wherever the question has three parts, i.e., three favorite foods, then a partner needs to match with only one part. Although this is time-consuming, it will actually save time in the future. Only after the clock is completed do you explain that these are clock appointments. That whenever you want the students to work in pairs you will announce, "Go to your four o'clock appointment and complete problems one and two," or "Meet with your nine o'clock appointment and label the countries on the map of Europe," or "Edit your paragraph with your twelve o'clock appointment." This permits smoother transitions, with no time lapse for choosing partners. Partners can change two or three times within a class period. It helps to have a master copy of partners available; students should paste their clock into a notebook that they will use all year.

- **Deck of Cards.** Keep a deck of playing cards on hand. Students can draw a card. Then all queens form a group, all fives, and so on.

- **Call Cards.** The use of call cards was explained as a housekeeping tip. Shuffle the cards and deal them out into groups. Leave the groups on your desk until the project is underway so that students who "forgot" when their name was called will be able to determine the answer smoothly. Of course, if the group assignment is going to require a distribution of talent or a break up of a monopoly, the teacher can "stack the deck" privately before dealing out the groups.

- **Rubrics.** All projects, especially group projects, require forethought and planning on the part of the teacher to provide purposeful guidance and to anticipate glitches.

Create a rubric or schedule of what is entailed in the project, criteria for accomplishment of each part, and the norms for grading.

- **Grading.** Devise a grading policy that includes student self-evaluation and assesses each student on his/her own merits and contribution to the group project. Involve the group in group-evaluation. This will mitigate against industrious students doing most of the work or being marked down because of unsatisfactory team effort.

MONITORING/REPORTING SELF-DISCIPLINE

Discussion of devising and advertising disciplinary procedures, rules, consequences, consistency, and stages of teacher correction has occurred elsewhere in this book. Now the focus will be on the need to monitor effort, conduct, homework, participation, and to report trouble areas to parents in a timely manner so that teacher, student, and parent can join forces in moving towards discipleship. There are many options for such reporting. For example, third-grade teacher Mary Ann Heavey of St. Leo the Great School (Fairfax, VA) uses a weekly Leo Bar to keep parents informed about their child's behavior choices:

> *"A **Leo Bar** is a strip of paper 1" x 6" divided into six one-inch squares. The first square has an image of Leo the Lion and the remaining squares are identified M-T-W-T-F for the days of the week. Each child is issued a Leo Bar at the beginning of each week. For responsible behavior choices a star is stamped in the square. If a student displays disruptive, unacceptable, irresponsible behavior, an OOPS! image is stamped in the day's square. At the end of the week parents are asked to sign the back of the Leo Bar and return it in the weekly folder if there was an OOPS! reported."*

Some teachers use professionally-sold homework notebooks. These are designed to help with student organization by providing a format for copying homework assignments down and recording test grades, etc. If a need arises to report concerns about effort, homework, or conduct, the teacher can make a brief notation in this book. This can be an effective tool for teacher-parent communication, since parents are expected to sign the book each day.

Another teacher from a departmental teaching group reports that she gives a reduced-size quarterly calendar to each student. It has brief, introductory remarks that define the criteria and expectation of effort, homework, and conduct. It also explains that all three teachers of the department will use this calendar. Ideally, the student block for each day will remain empty, signifying satisfactory performance. If, however, there is a need to report behavior, the teacher will merely put an E for effort, H for homework, or C for conduct, followed by the classroom number, i.e., C15 would translate as Conduct referral from the teacher of Room 15. At the end of each week the calendar is signed by the parents. Of course, parents are free to examine the calendar every day, if they wish. At the end of the quarter the calendar serves as the basis for determining report card grades for effort, conduct, and homework. It resolves the issue of a student who does well with "teacher A," but not with "teacher B." The report card grade represents the total picture. Both student and parent have constant and consistent notification of behavior choices, patterns, and pending trouble.

HOMEWORK:

- **Posting.** Homework should be posted prominently. Some teachers use a portion of the chalkboard for this purpose. They create a panel for the left side that lists each of the room subjects. Then, if an assignment is given, it is written on the chalkboard next to the subject name. I also maintain a homework notebook. The class secretary dates the work daily and copies the student assignments into it. Primary grades often use teacher-made homework weekly memos. By mid-year of grade two, students are probably capable of copying their own assignments.

- **Correcting.** Do not assign homework unless you will be checking it. Only very highly self-motivated students will continue doing homework once they know that chances are better than not that it will not be checked. In some classrooms, students leave notebooks or workbooks open to proper page and collect them one on top of another. The teacher or teacher aid then checks them at a convenient time. Some teachers have students self-correct assignments as the teacher walks through the room and verifies the completed assignment. Others use a single student notebook for all class work and homework. In those cases some teachers mark one group of books per day after school, yielding a weekly grade. Students use a paper clip to separate previously-examined work from new and they leave their books open on their desks when they leave for dismissal.

- **Expectations.** Be reasonable in the amount of work assigned and accurate in time expectations. Without announcing your purpose to the students, give them a typical homework assignment as class work and time it. When the majority have finished, that indicates how much time it takes the average student complete an assignment. When possible, anticipate assignments so parents and students can adapt school needs to their very harried schedules and students who need parent help have the opportunity to receive it.

- **Long Range Assignments, Projects & Contracts.** Use long-range assignments as tools to teach time-management, organizational skills, anticipation of deadlines, and good study habits. Break projects into segments that are due at different points. Teach skills that will be needed for a project before it is assigned. Maintain a monthly class assignment calendar to keep track of assignments and due dates. Avoid scheduling conflicts with departmental teachers: work out a balanced plan for long assignments, tests, and quizzes. When possible, let one project serve as a content grade as well as a grade for language arts and/or other areas of the curriculum. Streamline rather than multiply tasks.

A self-disciplined student is motivated internally to be respectful, responsible, and responsive. These traits are created in a climate of discipleship, in an environment that is marked by prudence, justice, fortitude, and temperance, in a culture characterized by practices such as charity, patience, goodness, kindness, long-suffering, mildness, fidelity, modesty, self-control, right-relationships, and laughter. The issues discussed in this chapter support such a climate. Considered in isolation, any one idea is merely interesting; in combination they form an environment for self-discipline and they structure the classroom for success. The Catholic educator is the key factor in establishing such principles.

Motivating Students to be Self-Disciplined

T HIS BOOK OFFERS the thesis that self-discipline is a dynamic process of becoming inner-directed, responsible, responsive, and reflective, thus supporting the skill of learning how to hear and recognize the will of God in daily choices. It is the premise of this book that self-discipline leads to discipleship, i.e., the desire to be like Jesus, and that discipline, as it has been defined in this book, is a biblically-based notion. A second premise of this book is that discipline is fostered in the Catholic school, as in any setting, through respectful attitudes, approaches, policies, behaviors, teachings, or conversations These lead students to a better understanding of God, themselves, and others. Finally, this book has suggested that when the interaction between teachers and students is instructive, respectful, proactive, positive, and directed towards the development of independence and intrinsic motivation, it contributes to the cultivation of discipleship and Christian character. It is in this spirit that this chapter offers to the reader the collected wisdom of teachers-in-the-field.

Catholic educators in California, Canada, Georgia, Pennsylvania, and Virginia participated in a workshop or credit course on the topic of cultivating a culture of discipline and discipleship in the Catholic school. The ideas expressed in the prologue and chapters one through four were presented to these teachers. Educators were invited to share one idea which reflected the definition that "discipline is an instructive, respectful, positive, and proactive process that motivates students to become inner-directed, responsible, responsive, and cooperative." The participants were also directed to: *"recommend a strategy, technique, or experience that motivates positive behavior and accountability in students."* These ideas are reproduced here. They are offered to fellow educators as examples of teacher motivation of students in self-discipline. Adaptation and revision are possible and, indeed, encouraged. Moreover, many ideas transcend the age or grade group from which they originated. Three examples are offered here to illustrate the possibility of adaptation, revision, flexibility, and universality.

1. In Chapter One, it was reported that eighth-grade teacher Julie Thompson of Holy Spirit School (Fairfield, CA) used six inch tracing letters to create a large banner that stretched across the front of her classroom. The letters spelled out the invitation: *"Let us remember that we are in the holy presence of God."* When her students need to re-focus, she merely points to the banner. That idea would be good in primary grades as well as high school classes. Kindergarten children could refer to a picture of Jesus. After explaining the concept, kindergarten students would understand that they are being reminded to refocus any time their teacher points to the picture. In any grade, a teacher could revise this idea by using a quotation that has particular relevance to the certain group of students.

2. First-grade teacher Tracie Noriega (St. Vincent Ferrer School, Vallejo, CA) offered an experience that can be adapted to every grade level. She wrote: *"At the beginning of the school year we sit together and discuss rules for the classroom. The students brainstorm and agree to the rules. They write the rules on a poster size paper together. Each student then signs the poster, agreeing to abide by the rules. This helps set the tone of caring for one another and helping each other to learn."*

3. Learning specialist, Sister Ann Mark, IHM (St. Cyril School, East Lansdowne, PA) shared a strategy that she uses when working with grades one through four. It is an example of the "stretch-ability" factor and would be helpful to teachers in any situation. Sister suggested: *"Be proactive! To avoid problems when students are put in a group, choose a craft stick from the teacher container of sticks to determine who goes first. The sticks are labeled, i.e., person closest to the door, closest birthday to the teacher's birthday, favorite animal, dad's or mom's first name, ABC order, month of birthday, etc. It helps to avoid problems while teaching other skills like directions, ABC order, thinking skills."* It also serves as a socializing agent.

The accounts that follow are discussion starters, not an exhaustive list of "do's." It is the hope of the author that faculties will examine their own practices and share them with others. Present colleagues with strategies, techniques, or experiences that motivate students to become self-disciplined. The teacher practices that follow are grouped into five categories:
- Practices that were suggested by administrators or specialty-area teachers and teachers who meet students in every grade or class;
- Practices of teachers in Grades Kindergarten, One and Two;
- Practices of teachers in Grades Three, Four, and Five;
- Practices of teachers in Grades Six, Seven, and Eight; and,
- Practices of teachers in High School.

Within each of these categories suggestions were listed alphabetically by the title that the teacher assigned to the practice.

Across Grades & Curricula

Acrostic Activity
Sandra Slavik (Computer Teacher, St. Mel School, Fair Oaks, CA)
Projects that foster positive self-image and dignity contribute to a respectful, cooperative atmosphere in the classroom. This

acrostic assignment has been a positive, proactive force among eighth-graders. As a computer class project, students design and word-process an acrostic, listing positive qualities about themselves for each letter of their first and last names. They may consult parents, teachers, and classmates. Generic descriptors like nice, funny, and cool are eliminated as possibilities. Finished products are shared and these qualities are referred to throughout the year. As a surprise at the end of the year the project is used as a cover for student writing portfolios and presented at the closing Graduate-Parent Dinner.

Action Plan
S. Thais Margiotta, IHM (Holy Family School, Harrisburg, PA)
To help a student to become responsible for his or her actions, divide a sheet of paper into four sections. Primary students will illustrate; upper grades will explain in writing: A. What happened? B. What were the consequences of the action? C. What will you do next time? D. What will be the consequences next time?

Appreciating Differences
Irene Kane (Guidance Counselor, St. Leo the Great Catholic School, Fairfax, VA)
I use the story of the ugly duckling as the basis for the lesson. (McKissack, P & McKissack F. (1986). *The Ugly Little Duckling. Children's Press Inc.*). However, I change the word "ugly" to "different" and have the students say "different" throughout the story as I give them a cue. We then color several ducks differently and discuss "different" as "being special." I have also used apples, showing that they are different on the outside but relatively the same on the inside.

Eyes! Ears!
Dave MacKenzie (Physical Education, Fr. Patrick Mercredi High School, Fort McMurray, Canada)
At the beginning of the class year, with students seated, I tell them, "When I say 'eyes!' you all stop physical movement, yell

'eyes!' and look at me. When I say 'ears!' you yell 'ears' and listen to me." It is a great way to teach students to be aware of their participation in the group, i.e., if they don't hear immediately, they will become aware of the cue because most others have stopped. Both teachers and students become whistle free. It works in a class where you have hearing-impaired students because the group stops all physical action. They can see the effect of the cue. Moreover, if you want to demonstrate a positive behavior or to review a rule, the teacher need not reorganize the group. Simply speak, demonstrate, and continue. It eliminates wasted time and the children love to scream!

Flash and Dash
Dave McKenzie (Fr. Patrick Mercredi High School, Fort McMurray, Canada)

This is a great review game; perfect for Fridays. It is high energy, allows maximum participation, and every child has a chance to be successful. This strategy can also be applied to any grade level or subject area. 1. Divide the class into two groups (but never boys vs. girls). Try to balance the academically stronger students, athletes, and those with out-going personalities. Let teams choose a team name and even make a banner. 2. Create a batting order for each team and let students to challenge each other. Sometimes the teacher will need to appoint the pairings as the game goes on. Everyone takes a turn. Shy students or injured students can be score keepers, judges, or board erasers. 3. Place two chairs and the judge at the back of the room facing the chalkboard. A player from each team sits on the designated chair. The teacher or facilitator announces a vocabulary word from the subject under review. The word is used in a sentence so that the students are sure of the word to be spelled. For example, *"The word is Canada. The United States is bordered on the north by Canada."* 4. Both players race to the front of the room and attempt to spell the word correctly. When finished, the player places the chalk in the ledge, crosses his or her arms across the chest, and faces the judge who is sitting in the back of the room. Whoever is finished first and has correctly spelled the word gets to answer a review question for five points. The loser sits down with the team. The defeated player must receive two "nice try-high fives" from teammates or his team loses one point. 5. A question is asked of a student, for instance, "What is the capital of Canada?" If the student gets the question right, five points are added to the team score. If the student answers incorrectly, the other team can try the answer for three points. If the original student wants to discuss the question with teammates, a correct answer yields a reduced score of three points. If the team answer is wrong, the opposition team can steal it for two points. 6. Repeat until all players have had at least one turn. *Special Rules*: 1. This game only serves as a review if everyone listens. When the teacher says, "Peace," you have three seconds to be silent or you lose point from your team score. 2. No notes or texts can be open. 3. If spellers tie, i.e., finish writing the vocabulary word correctly at exactly the same time, use "rock/paper/scissors," a card draw, or dice to break the tie. 4. No put downs or teasing. 5. Cheering is allowed. 6. No foreign objects in the path to the board. Shoe laces must be tied.

Growing in Values & Virtues
S. Kathleen Marie Metz, IHM (Our Lady of Fatima School, Bensalem, PA)

The administration and faculty select nine values or virtues to emphasize for the school year. Because students know and are accountable to practice all nine virtues on every day of the year, teachers respond to "teachable moments" as they surface, while the school community highlights one virtue a month for discussion and celebration. Practical definitions and ideas are discussed in each classroom, referred to at Morning Assembly, and posted on bulletin boards. Teachers try to "catch" students practicing the value/virtue during the month and "Student of the Month" recognition is based on this criterion. In May, classes contribute to create a large display of the virtues that Mary demonstrated. Each child colors a paper flower on which he names the value/virtue that he grew in during the year. The combination of the student flowers creates a garden. At the end of the school year, students assemble for a final blessing. Each grade is "blessed" (commissioned) to practice one of the virtues throughout the summer.

I Know Who You Are!
Connie Benne (Computer Teacher, St. Basil School, Vallejo, CA)
     I try to use the first name of each student during class time. It could be a greeting at the door or recognition of being on task. All students come to the computer lab at least weekly.

Let It Go to Grow
Kathy Farr (Math and Science Teacher, Grades 4-8, St. Mel School, Fair Oaks, CA)
     When a child is upset over poor progress, discuss the situation. Together find the cause, if possible, and consider ways to improve or avoid future frustration. Then, advise the student to "let it go." Do not dwell on or fret about the situation.

P.E. Picks
Stephanie Rossup (Grades K-8 Physical Education, St. Mel School, Fair Oaks, CA)
     In the gymnasium students are seated in rows and have assigned "self-space spots." At the end of the period, the row that worked together the most cooperatively, positively, and stayed on task can choose the closing activity in which all students participate. If wall space permits, create a visual grid of "self-space spots." Across the front or back wall place placards of letters A through F. On the adjacent wall place placards of numbers 1 through 6, etc. This visual organizational tool contributes to self-regulatory behavior.

Peer Teacher
Marjorie Booth (Reading Teacher, Grades 1-4, St. Mel School, Fair Oaks, CA)
     I work with small groups of children for reading class. Though few in number, they can easily become distracted or fail to pay attention. To refocus them, I ask a student who is paying attention to lead the class. This student can select another student

to read, keep score in a vocabulary lesson, or perform some task that gives that student authority. I have found that the students focus attention on their peer teacher.

Personal Contracts
Racette Griffin (Special Needs, Grades 9-12, Fr. Patrick Mercredi High School)

Personal contracts consist of four parts: (a) concerns, (b) goals, (c) consequences, and (d) action items. When behavior occurs which warrants a conference between teacher, student, parent, and administrator, I use the Personal Contract. Before the meeting, the student fills out a blank contract that lists of each of the four contract headings. The student considers the problem with his behavior, what his goal is in this class, what he thinks is a justified consequence for a particular behavior, and what the teacher, parent, and administrator can do to assist him in achieving his goal. After the student has thought about these things, he and I discuss the contract and try to deal with any discrepancies before the conference. Otherwise, this is addressed at the conference. It is important that the student feels that he is being heard and has a say in his behavior, consequence, and goals. At the conference, with the assistance of the student, I review the contract with the parents and administrator. Many students are afraid to lead the conference and the key is not to embarrass the student but to make him accountable for his academic success. At the end of the conference, everyone signs the contract to signify their commitment. If the student breaks the contract, I take it out of his personal file and show him the consequence. The next day is a new day. I have had a tremendous amount of success with these contracts. They give students a sense of ownership and accountability with their education. In many cases, the students are harder on themselves than I would be. It helps to eliminate the idea that the teacher is always the bad guy!

Personal Responsibility Action Plan
S. Anne B. McGuire, IHM (IHM Professional Development Center, Philadelphia, PA)

The principal facilitates this strategy for a student at-risk when the efforts of the teacher with the parents and the child are at an impasse. The principal begins the conference by establishing the purpose of meeting: to identify the area of difficulty and what each person can do to help the student succeed. 1. A conference, initiated by the principal, requires the teacher(s), one parent, and the child to be in attendance. 2. In a non-judgmental manner, the teacher describes the child's action to the parent. Facts are presented, with dates and examples. 3. The student has the opportunity to present his/her thoughts and concerns. The parent also has this opportunity. 4. The principal presents concerns for the child and his/her opportunities to succeed. All information is recorded on a conference sheet. 5. All agree on a *Personal Responsibility Action Plan*. (A) What will the child do and when? (B) What will the parent do and when? (C) What will the teacher do and when? 6. A follow-up conference to evaluate progress is scheduled for two weeks later. 7. Each person present signs the Action Plan and receives a copy. 8. Progress is evaluated at the next conference.

Real World Learning: Credit Cards
Nora Facchiano (Grade 2 and ESP Director, St. Mark School, Hyattsville, MD)

As in real life parents much have good credit to be able to have the privilege of buying a car or a house, I teach the children that they, too, must have good credit to earn extra privileges in the classroom. Each month every child receives a new Credit Card that is about 4"x4" in the shape of a seasonal image, i.e., pumpkin for October. A seasonal mini reward sticker is placed on the credit card for each reward. The behaviors that I reward are: (1) first three to begin a new task assigned, (2) first three to unpack and begin the day's work, (3) first to follow a new direction, (4) the first one or two to come to order after free activity, (5) for those who get teacher notes and homework signed. At the end of the month each child totals the stickers on the credit card. The top three (VIP's) and the three most improved (MI's) or teacher's choice (TC's) win. These names are posted and for a month those students have special privileges such as using the classroom loft for a reading and/or listening area, use of computers during break times, building an item at the wood bench and keeping it. If a student looses credit on the card by misplacing it, he must accept the loss. Just as in real life, if you do not take care of things you will lose them.

Three Ounces of Prevention
Mary Pettitt (St. Adelaide School, San Bernardino, CA)

Ounce #1: I have a custom-made rubber stamp that says: Quality ___, Neatness ___, Total Grade ____. I have only to use this a few times at the beginning of the year in order to have neatness quickly become a habit. *Ounce #2*: I send home a weekly "sign and return" folder. It contains heavily weighted assignments, with each marked off on a quarter/trimester grade page. It also reports work that was not turned in. All work must be turned in or I telephone home. This is a regular parent communication. Parents appreciate it and children learn accountability from it. *Ounce #3*: On papers that have high scores I write the phrase, "High Score" or "Highest Score," especially if it belongs to a student who struggles. It is amazing the way pride motivates students to try harder and to succeed.

Timely Transition
S. Elaine Brookes, IHM (Supervisor of Elementary Schools, Immaculata, PA)

Transition time between lessons, subjects, or activities is a critical point in the classroom and requires good management and practical strategies. This time is best used by singing, reciting poetry, or repeating some aspect of the curriculum, i.e., times tables, chart of percent/fraction equivalents, parts of speech, states and capitals, etc.. Employing this technique will provide a smooth transition and keep students focused.

Practices Suggested by Teachers of Grades K, 1 and 2

ABC Chart (A Better Choice) *Advice for Parents*
S. Angela Mastrangelo (Grade K-1, Immaculate Conception School, Levittown, PA)

The following strategy has been used successfully in several home settings as a major component in the behavior development of five and six year old children who display a high degree of resistance to obeying parents and rules at home. *Materials*: 1 poster board, 4 pages of a large calendar, attractive stickers, colored markers, glue. *Strategy*: 1. Lead the child to an understanding of what a choice is. 2. Help the child gather pictures of six good choices. 3. Place the pictures in collage form on the poster board. 4. Create an *ABC Chart* by printing the child's name at the top of each calendar page and label it "ABC." 5. Use one page a week to focus child's daily attention on positive choices. 6. Encourage child to make good choices across environments—home, school, and at play. 7. Each time the child makes "A Better Choice," award the child a sticker placed in the appropriate calendar block. 8. At the end of four weeks, celebrate the child's successes.

Caught Being Good
Joan Osborne (Grade 1, St. Basil School, Vallejo, CA)

I have a poster on the front chalkboard that says "Caught Being Good." Throughout the day, as I see children showing acts of kindness, following class rules, making good choices, I put their names on the chalkboard. I also draw attention to the fact that their name is going on the board and I thank them for their good choice. I award a sticker at the end of the day.

Class Rules
Tracie Noriega (Grade 1, St. Vincent Ferrer School, Vallejo, CA)

At the beginning of the school year the students and I discuss rules for the classroom. The students brainstorm and agree to the rules. They write the rules on a poster-size paper together. Each student then signs the poster, agreeing to abide by the rules. This helps set the tone of caring for one another and helping each other to learn.

Count the Stars
Sr. Helen Teresa, IHM (Grade 1, St. Aloysius Academy, Bryn Mawr, PA)

Whenever you "catch" a child or the class being cooperative, draw a star on the chalkboard. At the end of the day the students are thrilled to see the number of stars that they have earned together.

First Grade Magic
Sr. Helen Teresa, IHM (Grade 1, St. Aloysius Academy, Bryn Mawr, PA)

When things get a little chaotic I turn to the wall and announce, "First Grade Magic." Then I count to five. When I turn around, all are seated and eyes are on me to begin anew. Of course, this strategy needs explanation and practice before it becomes operational.

French Fried Behavior
Sr. William Catherine Brannen (Grade 2, St. Joachim School, Philadelphia, PA)

Ask a fast food restaurant to donate one empty, new french fry box for each student. Label them with student names and clip three clothespins onto each box. If a child misbehaves, the child removes one french fry from the box and pays the consequence, i.e., one fry: the student loses five minutes of recess; two fries: the student loses the entire recess; three fries: a note is sent to the parents. Each student who ends the school day in possession of all three fries collects a celebration ticket. Ten tickets can be traded in for a prize from the Celebration Box.

God Tools
Dan Trzebiatowski (Kindergarten, St. Bernard School, Tracy, CA)

I always try to 'preach' that we do right things simply because they are the right things to do. We do not do things for a reward. I give only non-material recognition, i.e., extra recess, or not having to color a paper. The students are not rewarded for everything. I teach them that God gives you the tools but you must do the work.

Good Listeners
Sally Muratori (Kindergarten Assistant, St. Basil School, Vallejo, CA)

We have a poster in our classroom and the teacher uses this poster to remind the students about good behavior. The poster reads: *Rules for Good Listeners: Ears Listening, Eyes Watching, Hands Still, Feet Quiet, Lips Closed.* Each phrase has a picture of a cute character demonstrating the rule. When it is necessary, the teacher will tap on the poster to remind the students of the rules. It is a respectful, instructive, and effective way to re-focus kindergarten children.

Jesus Comes to Me
Mary Frontier (Grade 1, St. Mel School, Fair Oaks, CA)

During religion class I frequently tell students to think of a time when they have recently felt happy, felt a new understanding of something they previously did not understand, felt joy, felt loved, were hugged, felt the feeling of someone sharing with them, etc. I explain that these are ways of God being present. I have them draw a picture to illustrate their experience. They call the picture, *Jesus Comes Daily* or *God Loves Me*. I try to do this several times each week.

Leo Bar
Mary Ann Heavey (Grade 3, St. Leo the Great, Fairfax, VA)

A *Leo Bar* is a 1" x 6" strip of paper divided into six one-inch squares. The first square has an image of Leo the Lion and the remaining squares are identified M-T-W-T-F for the days of the week. Each child is issued a Leo Bar at the beginning of each week. For responsible behavior choices a star is stamped in the square. If a student displays disruptive, unacceptable, irresponsible behavior, an OOPS! image is stamped in the day's square. At the end of the week parents are asked to sign the back of the Leo Bar and return it in the weekly folder if there was an OOPS! reported.

Musical Silence
S. Anne Pierre Reed, IHM (Learning Support Teacher, Grades 1-4, St. Martin of Tours, Philadelphia, PA)

The goal is to make the transition from recess to the next class. Teach and practice the following procedure: (1) Ring a bell to signal clean up; (2) Turn on calming music. Students go to the next instruction area and put their heads down until the music stops; (3) When the music stops, the teacher or aide begins the next period.

Order to Groups
S. Ann Mark, IHM (Grades 1-4, St. Cyril School, East Lansdowne, PA)

Be creative in forming student groups. Prepare seasonal die-cuts or store-bought shapes, i.e., witches, ghosts, cats, pumpkins. Write numbers and letters on the back. Laminate them for continued use. Then when you want to form groups, pass out the items. Announce, "All witches in a group," or "Witches and ghosts with number "x" on the back," or "with letter "x" on the back," or "All ones together," or "All a's together," etc. It is quick, easy, and fun.

Pick a Stick
S. Ann Mark, IHM (Grades 1-4, St. Cyril School, East Lansdowne, PA)

To avoid problems when students are put in a group, choose a craft stick from the container to determine who goes first. The sticks are labeled, i.e., person closest to the door, closest birthday to the teacher's birthday, favorite animal, dad's or mom's first name, ABC order, month of birthday, etc. It helps to avoid problems while teaching other skills like directions, ABC order, thinking skills, etc.

Reading Reports
Elaine Moura (Grade 2, St. Mel School, Fair Oaks, CA)

Periodically I give a Reading Report to each child when they have read orally during reading group time. I write their name on a small piece of paper and write a sentence complementing them on their reading, i.e., knowing all words, using expression, or pausing for punctuation. I sign with a happy face and add a sticker. Before the group leaves I always thank them for reading to me and I let them know how much I enjoyed it.

Recipe for Teacher Assistant
Herlina B. Cruz (Grade 1, Teacher Assistant, St. Vincent Ferrer School, Vallejo, CA)

At the start of each class day be emotionally present and alert to teacher needs and help in any way possible. If the teacher gives explanations or discussions, make sure that the students are listening and following the directions given. Circulate among the students regularly. Be a quiet force that assists students to focus, re-focus, or to stay on task.

Self-Control Marbles
Michele Doss (Grade 1, St. Leo the Great School, Fairfax, VA)

I have discovered that my students have wonderful self-control under my supervision, but, once out of sight, they can be quite unruly. I want them to understand that self-control should always to be practiced, no matter where they are. I use a marble system. When my students receive an unsolicited compliment about their behavior from any adult other than me, we add a marble to our *SELF CONTROL JAR*. We have a pre-set goal line on the jar. When we reach that goal we celebrate with a game day. Everyone brings a towel and board game to share. We sit on the floor, play games, watch a movie, have a special snack, and celebrate our growth in self-control.

Spot
Joann Donati (Grades K-3, St. Joseph Regional Academy, Jim Thorpe, PA)

Post a drawing of a dog with removable spots on the wall. Label each spot with a student name. Hang the spots on the dog with names showing. Place your class rules and consequences beside the dog. For example: 1. Verbal warning 2. Turn your spot over. 3. Bring your spot to the teacher desk and (a) time out or

(b) write a three sentences of explanation and get it signed by a parent. 4. Go to the principal. Telephone home. Each day every student starts over. All spots are on the dog with names showing to begin the school day.

Star Corner
Sr. Betty Bailey, IHM (Grade 2, St. Pius X School, Broomall, PA)

This strategy was developed to work on classroom behavior. When the children come into the classroom in the morning and follow the procedure, a star is placed on the chalkboard in the *Star Corner*. Throughout the day if procedures and rules are followed, stars are added, with a maximum of five stars. For each star a minute is added to recess the next day. If the class receives five stars from Monday through Thursday, a special treat is given on Friday, i.e., extra DEAR time (Drop Everything And Read), play a group game, or partner game, etc.

Star Power
Sr. Therese Elizabeth, IHM (Grade 1, St. John the Baptist School, Manayunk, PA)

Children are given small paper stars for demonstrating positive behaviors, such as good listening, helping another student, keeping desk and materials organized, etc. At given intervals stars are traded for small prizes. Each prize is labeled with a star value. Children learn responsibility by keeping their stars in a given place and knowing when they can trade them in for prizes. The stars are also a reminder to the students that they are all stars that shine brightly with each good act.

Sticker Chart
Lucille Semeran & Kay Roberts (Kindergarten, St. Leo the Great, Fairfax, VA)

We begin the Sticker Chart once classroom expectations have been introduced and discussed with the students. 1. Each child is given a seasonal sticker chart, i.e., an apple, pumpkin, or turkey that they cut out of construction paper. 2. A child receives stickers daily for following classroom rules and performing acts of kindness. 3. A child loses stickers if rules are not followed. 4. At the end of each month, the stickers are counted. Each sticker is worth one cent. At the beginning of the year, each family sends a roll of pennies with the child. 5. Each child counts the number of pennies they have earned and puts them into their bank (a baby food jar). The children count individually with the teacher, so that we can assess their counting skills 6. We set up our school store at the end of the month. We have items that are donated by parents and even parents of former students. Items in the store may include, coloring books, crayons, stickers, McDonalds toys, Burger King prizes, etc. The toys are placed in eight different boxes. Each box is priced differently, ranging from one to twenty cents. Children work individually with the teacher when purchasing their items to figure out payment. They are welcome to spend all of their pennies or save some for the next month. 7. The children respond very well to this system. It works beautifully and we have found the parents equally responsive.

Stop Light
Lauri Power (Gr. 2, Holy Spirit School, Fairfield, CA)
Sabrina Thornton (Kindergarten, St. Basil School, Vallejo, CA)

Construct a *traffic light* poster. From top to bottom arrange circles or paper/plastic plates of red, yellow, and green. Around the circumference of the green circle, clip a snap clothespin for each student, labeled it with their name and alphabetical number. Arrange the clothespins in alphabetical order. Below the *traffic light* publish your class rules and the consequences for choosing to break a rule. For example: 1. GREEN light: All is well! Meeting expectations! 2. Verbal warning. 3. YELLOW light: Caution; Slow Down! Settle Down! Move name clothespin to yellow light. 4. RED light: Stop! Move name to red light; be removed from activity. *(If age appropriate, write three sentences at recess that recount the situation. Get a parent signature for homework.)* 5. Severe disruption: Go to the Principal. Parent contact follows. To keep parents informed about their child's behavior in the classroom, create a small monthly calendar. Attach it to the weekly communication envelope. Use a color-coded stamp to indicate daily behavior, i.e., green, yellow, or red.

Thumbs Up When You're Ready

Joanne York (Kindergarten, St. Mel School, Fair Oaks, CA)

Objective: To re-focus and quiet children without having to raise your voice to get attention. *Strategy*: At the beginning of the year, I tell students that when they see my thumb raised, it means that it is time to be quiet and listen for directions. I stand quietly and wait until everyone is ready. By the end of the year, children do it themselves as a signal to me that it is either too noisy or that they are ready for what is coming next.

What Would Jesus Do?

Claudette Fiddler (Grade 1, Father Beauregarde School, Alberta, Canada)

Make a tree the central image on a bulletin board. Put a picture of Jesus in the middle and the words, *"What would Jesus do?"* as the title. Establish a theme for each month, i.e., apples, pumpkins, Christmas trees, etc. Create a theme card for each student and place the cards near the tree. Whenever a student does something kind for another, he puts his name card on the tree. At the end of the day the teacher asks a student to put a small sticker on each name card posted on the tree (or punch a hole) and the name cards are taken down and ready for the next day. At some point during the day the teacher can ask the student what he did for another and offer some positive feedback. At the end of the month the name card goes home. The students enjoy filling their name cards with stickers and doing their kind acts as well.

You Are a Reflection of Jesus

Nanette Speaker (Grade 2, St. Bernard School, Tracy, CA)

When conflict arises, after sorting out the details, I ask the student who hit, tripped, pushed, or was unkind if they would treat Jesus that way. The answer is always no! I reply, "Then why you would do that to 'so and so'? We are all a part of Jesus." It has been effective in avoiding conflict because it makes them think twice about being unkind or hurting someone else. I consistently place before the class the greatest commandment: *Love God and love your neighbor as yourself.*

Practices Suggested by Teachers of Grades 3, 4 and 5
Assignment Collecting Procedure
Barbara Joyce (Grade 4, St. Mel School, Fair Oaks, CA)

Each subject area has a tray on the counter in the classroom. Before students arrive for the day I pull the subject trays to the edge of the counter for assignments that are due. When the students enter the classroom they get ready for the day; this includes turning in homework assignments. Students are reminded visually by the seeing the subject trays. As a result, I have few missing assignments. I have the blessing of having an aide who checks in all homework at 8:30 AM. Out of thirty-seven students, one or two might miss homework. We compliment the students on their responsible behavior.

Bonus Points
Kevin Crossin (Grade 5, St. Leo the Great School, Fairfax, VA)

This program starts at the beginning of the school year. After classroom rules are established, students earn a bonus point for demonstrating behavior consistent with these rules. I tell them the behavior that I like while handing them the Bonus Point Card, i.e., "I really like the way you got your books out quickly and quietly." (My cards are 2"x 2" squares of paper that bear the title "BONUS POINT!" and the statement, "Thank you for following Classroom rules." At the bottom is the title "Name" and a line on which the student writes his/her name.) I am very generous with points at the beginning of the year. As time goes by I expect students to internalize the behaviors and I hand out the point cards less frequently. Whenever I need to quiet the class, simply pulling out the cards brings attention to me. In the fifth grade they keep the cards and are responsible for them. I do not replace lost cards. At the end of the quarter, students turn in cards for rewards. At the beginning of the year the students vote on a list of things they would like to "buy" with the points, i.e., lunch in the room with the teacher, sitting at the teacher's desk, time on the class computer. I set the "prices" for the items. The student turns in the points, and receives a certificate for the item. I try to set prices so that each student can buy at least one item.

Celebration of Self Mastery
Sheri Hunt (Grade 3, St. Mel School, Fair Oaks, CA)

Students seated in groups or rows become a "team" for the month. Each team creates its own name. Throughout the month the team is awarded points for various self-reliant behavior, i.e., having books open to correct page, getting ready for lunch or dismissal in an efficient manner, working quietly, etc. At the end of the month the team with the most points enjoys a Celebration of Self-Mastery, i.e., a Popsicle, extra library time, or lunch with teacher. Teams change monthly. This approach promotes self-discipline, cooperative learning, and teamwork.

Common Good
Gwen Gaulke (Grades K-3, Teacher Aide, St. Mel, Fair Oaks, CA)

During yard duty award stickers when you observe students being kind to others, picking up trash, offering to help others, etc.

Don't Strike Out
N. Waldron (Grade 4, St. Leo the Great School, Fairfax, VA)

Clearly establish desirable behaviors in the areas of responsibility, organization, and behavior. Post a "Strike Zone" in your classroom (this is a sheet of paper with a square marked off for each student. Post a new sheet each week). If the student commits an infraction he/she writes it in his/her box. Three strikes in the course of a week results in a lunchtime detention, when the student writes a 100-word essay on responsibility, etc. Strikes are also noted on a weekly progress report which is signed by parents. At the end of the week a clear box earns "effort points." Effort points can be earned in other ways. These can be used to modify behavior and individualized for special needs. Effort points are never taken away and the personal accumulation of ten warrants a small prize.

Get Your Name in Lights
Sr. Hannah Miller, IHM (Grade 5, St. Aloysius Academy, Bryn Mawr, PA)

Tape a string of lights to the board or use pins to create a frame of lights on a cork board. Write each student's name or use peel off labels. Start the week with all names in lights. Clearly express the hope that all names stay there! Determine a behavior or class goal and only remove the names of "violators" or "slackers." Another variation is to begin the week with an empty frame and add names as the week progresses.

Give Me Five!
Anonymous (Fort McMurray Catholic School District, Alberta, Canada)

Post a drawing of a hand. Label each of the five fingers with the following directions: (1) Eyes Looking; (2) Ears Listening; (3) Mouth Quiet; (4) Hands Still; (5) Feet Still. After teaching the concept, use the expression "Give me five!" to refocus an individual or a class.

Homework Heroes
Sr. Carolyn Ann Bennett, IHM (Grade 5, St. James Catholic School, Savannah, GA)

Create a class chart that lists each student. Label the information blocks with dates. Each day of the week the students can earn a star for completion of homework assignments. At the end of the week, students who have earned a star for each day get a coupon that qualifies them for a chance drawing from the Treasure Chest. The items in the Treasure Chest come from a "dollar store" and are donated by the parents. I pull out coupons from two boys and two girls and they choose a prize. All the other coupons remain all year and the children keep adding to the jar throughout the year. Students with missed assignments come to a Lunch Club class. I discuss with them the reasons they did not complete their work. If this problem continues, I contact their parents.

How's Your Day?

Kathleen Hedrick (Grade 4, St. Bernard School, Tracy, CA)

Something I do every day to let my students know that I care about them and their feelings is to find out what kind of day they are having before we even start school. As I take roll, I have them indicate what kind of day they are having by showing me 1, 2, 3, or 4 fingers as they say "here." One finger indicates they are having a very good day; 2 is a good day; 3 is a not so good day; and 4 is really poor. I smile, wink, or give the thumbs up to children with the 1 and 2 responses and try to say something encouraging to those who respond with a 3 or 4, i.e., "I hope it gets better," or "Breathe in God's love and breathe out the hurt." Sometimes I ask what is wrong. Being able to say that the day is not so good and to hear others say they have had the same problems seems to make them feel a little better. I also let them know what kind of day I am having, but usually only if I am off to a really bad start. Then they know that my patience and tolerance level is low and they try their very best to follow our rules. I tell them I need an attitude change and if they smile at me that will help me. Teachers have bad days, too.

I Am Queen!

Mary Holtz (Grade 5, St. Mel School, Fair Oaks, CA)

When a subject is to begin I write what is needed on the board. I stand to the side of the class and watch students gather materials, i.e.. book, homework, pen, folder, etc. Then I walk to the front and center of the room and say, "Queen Mary is ready. Let us begin. You are my loyal subjects."

Let's Go Home

Sr. Edward Mary, IHM (Grade 4 Special Needs, St. Matthew School, Philadelphia, PA)

Teach a procedure for peaceful dismissal for change of class. For instance, I call my procedure, "Let's Go Home." H=Pack up materials; O=Quiet and prepare to pray. Recite Class Prayer; M=Line up for blessing with Holy Water. I bless them on their foreheads; E=Children walk quietly to their classroom or destination.

Life Skills for Students
Sharon Veguary (Grade 3, St. Basil School, Vallejo, CA)

Throughout the school year I talk about specific life skills. Different life skills are discussed daily, i.e., courage, responsibility, organization, cooperation, flexibility, effort, caring, curiosity, a sense of humor, patience, common sense, friendship, problem-solving, perseverance, initiative, and integrity. I weave the life skills into communication, i.e., "Thank you, John, for being so honest. I appreciate that you use the life skill of integrity." The life skill can also be used as a tool to get students to reflect. For instance, if a student has been very impatient, the teacher can direct the child to write sentences that illustrate how she/he can display more patience in a future situation.

Now or Later
Sally Stone (Grade 5, St. Basil School, Vallejo, CA)

Homework is work to be done at home and then placed in the appropriate "subject box" the next morning at school before class prayer time. If a student's assignment is missing from the box, an immediate consequence results. The student uses recess time to complete the assignment.

Picking Sticks
Sally Stone (Grade 5, St. Basil School, Vallejo, CA)

We keep two coffee cups in our classroom. One is filled with popsicle sticks. Each of these sticks bears a student name. Whenever I feel that fairness is required, we pick sticks to choose which student will participate in an activity. Once a stick is chosen it is placed in the second coffee cup until all students have had a turn.

Post It Magic
Mary Savina Byczek (Grade 5, St. Leo the Great School, Fairfax, VA)

I love to use small "post it" notes to let a child know how special he or she is to me. I usually prepare my "messages" the night before; when I come to school the next day I place them strategically inside books, lockers, and desks. Sometimes I'll stick them in places where I know that the student will find it to be a real surprise! Each message is always positive and only a few notes are given weekly. My biggest surprise occurred when I attended the high school graduation of a former student. She told me that she had in her wallet a "magic note" that I had written when she was in my fifth grade.

Transition Time Tunes
Tina Brown (Grade 5, St. Bernard School, Tracy, CA)

As a first year teacher I found it difficult to transition in between subjects. The noise from books, papers, talking, and desks opening and closing was too much! I turned on some Christian music (Fernando Ortega, *This Good Day*) to cover the noise. Not only did the students stop talking; they began singing and wanted the lyrics. Now the students know that they have until the end of the song to be prepared for the next subject.

Practices Suggested by Teachers of Grades 6, 7, 8

Are You Ready Quiz
Victor Steel (Grades 7-12, Fr. McMurray Catholic Schools, Canada)

The first few minutes of any class often sets the pace for the rest of the time. After years of wasting a few minutes each day and trying to settle the noise level down I changed it all with my "Are You Ready Quiz." The quiz is completed everyday as the first thing said after the bell has rung. I begin with a quiet statement to the students of "Are you ready . . .?" and then I ask a question that is based on something that we did in the previous class and requires a one or two word answer. The question is not repeated nor are there more than a few moments given to complete the answer. The answer is written in one box on a page that a grid of twenty squares. The grid paper is renewed each month. Each correct answer is worth 5%; the whole is worth 100%. Students are responsible for picking up their own grid answer sheet as they come into the class, waiting quietly for the question, seated with a pen, and knowing what went on the day before so that indeed they are "ready" to learn.

Better Choices Form
Carolyn Maher (Grade 6, St. Vincent Ferrer School, Vallejo, CA)

Aim: To lead a student to "own" behavior and to learn how to predict the consequence of behavior before making a choice. *Procedure*: After a poor behavior choice has been made, give the student a form of 3-4 questions which include: (1) "What could you have chosen to do instead of the behavior choice you made?" and, (2) "How do you feel about yourself as a result of your choice?" Discuss the responses and write a teacher comment on the back of the form. File the form. Invite parents into the discussion if poor behavior continues.

C.E.O. (Creative Education Opportunity) Book for Creative Writing
S. Mary Anne Bolger, IHM (Grade 6, Sacred Heart School, Philadelphia, PA)

Students have a special notebook for writing. Each morning a "mini" writing topic is written on the chalkboard so that students can get started on their writing immediately upon entry to class. This activity focuses the children and helps to set the tone for the day. Before the Language Arts lesson, a few students read their writings. By the end of the week, all students will have read one of their "originals."

Class Attention
Marilyn Carmichael (Grade 8, St. Basil School, Vallejo, CA)

When the class becomes talkative I call out the name of a student who is quiet and say something like, "John, I like the way you are sitting and listening," or "Margie, I admire your industry and appreciate your cooperation." Generally, the class quiets down and looks toward the student named.

Eye to Eye, Hand to Hand, Person to Person
Suzanne Smoky (Grade 7, St. Mel School, Fair Oaks, CA)

When students leave my classroom at the end of the day I shake hands with each one. While the day may have gone by with little attention to any particular student, we end the day by looking into each other's eyes, touching each other's hands, and acknowledging each other's presence in our lives. The first month is pretty funny and awkward, but it catches on and knits us together.

Focal Point
Julie Thompson (Grade 8, Holy Spirit School, Fairfield, CA)

We use 6-inch tracing letters to create a large banner in the classroom that says, *"Let us remember that we are in the holy presence of God."* When students need to re-focus, merely point to the banner.

Freeze
Lisa Andersen (Grade 6, St. Bernard School, Tracy, CA)

When I need to get attention during group activities I count out loud backwards from five to one. Then I say "You're at Freeze." The students freeze in whatever position they are in until I say, "Un-freeze." At that point all attention is focused on me and I give whatever instructions are needed.

Getting to Know You
S. Roseanne M. Rodgers, IHM (Grades 7-8, Our Lady of Fatima School, Secane, PA)

The opening days of school are less hectic for me since I have learned to arrange seating before I meet the classes. Rather than using alphabetical order, I tend to reverse the process so that the last may be first. I make adjustments during the first week of school so that taller or smaller students may be accommodated. This system assists me when I am dealing with four classes. My seating plans are laminated. I can easily check attendance. It is a great asset for learning student names quickly.

Group Work
Eileen Walsh (Junior High Social Studies, St. Basil School, Vallejo, CA)

Soon after the students enter the classroom I turn on the overhead projector which displays the goals, objectives, and assignments for the class period. Usually students work in groups of three and the groupings change for each chapter. Group work has a set of rules to follow. For example, students may not talk outside their group without permission. If they do, they work alone that day. If a student continues to disrespect the group rule, he or she completes the chapter work independently, but can return to group work with the next chapter assignment. Group size and participants change according to need. In the second semester student may submit charts of group membership with the understanding that I may make changes if students do not work well together.

How is Your Day?
Anonymous (Grades 5-8, St. Mel School, Fair Oaks, CA)

Purchase or construct a pocket chart with one pocket per student. Label the pocket with student name or code number. In each pocket place four cards in the following sequence: green, yellow, red, and blue. Discuss class goals related to cooperation, respect, and responsibility. Elicit examples of positive choices and explanations of the harm caused by negative choice from students. Explain the pocket chart system of accountability: A Green Card indicates that all is well; a Yellow Card gives a first warning; a Red Card indicates that the student must write up what he or she will do differently to alter the course of a poor behavior choice; and a Blue Card indicates that a parent will be notified.

Jesus Focus
Terence P. Rocca (Junior High, St. Bernard School, Tracy, CA)

I have used the following to refocus a class without having to break off the lecture or lesson plan: 1. If the class needs to get on track I simply say, "God is good." They respond, "Always." I then say, "Always." They respond, "God is good." 2. Above the statue of Mary, I have a sign that reads: *"Jesus is the heartbeat of our lives."* I merely point to the sign and the class refocuses.

Oops Book!
S. Mary C. McNulty, IHM (Grades 4-8, St. Ephrem School, Bensalem, PA)

This suggestion aids self-government and provides an effective tool for tracking student effort and homework. (1) In a teacher copybook or binder use one page for each student. Write the student name at the top of the page to begin the school year. Label the next line as first quarter or first trimester. Then create three columns labeled: date, infraction, and signature. (2) If the student misbehaves and your "look" or direction is not effective, or if the child has incomplete homework, you simply tell the student to sign the book. Students write the date and infraction in their own writing. When they complete the work they bring it to you at a designated time and you initial it. They are responsible for bringing it to you. If a student accumulates three or more entries, you may want to issue a detention or demerit. For most students it will not get to this point. If a troublesome pattern develops, duplicate the page from the book for a parent conference. (3) At the end of the marking period I recognize diligence and effort by issuing a homework pass to students who have no entries in the book. (4) I repeat the procedure for each marking period. Each quarter or trimester provides a fresh start and the possibility of earning a homework pass. This technique avoids argumentation. When a student says, "Oops, I forgot!" or "Oops, I can't find it!" I simply say, "Sign the Oops Book!"

Preparedness and Structured Classroom
Diane Zielke (Grade 5, St. Anne School, Alberta Canada)

I find that I have fewer discipline problems if I am prepared for my classes and the students have a structured environment. For example, the students know that when they come into the classroom in the morning to organize themselves; they then begin to read silently until announcement time. They do this everyday and it cuts down on discipline problems. The same is true for each change of subject. There is a ritual for each that directs focus and readiness. The structure provides a student comfort level because they know what my expectations are. My signal for getting student attention is to shut off the lights. At the beginning of every lesson I let them know how much time will be given for the assignment. If they finish early they may complete other work or read silently. If they are not finished in the time frame they know they must complete the assignment as homework.

Redemption Day
Patricia M. McCormack (Grades 7-8, St. Simon School, Los Altos, CA)

I use the first few days of school to establish routines, expectations, formats for student class work, homework, and quizzes, etc. Throughout the first month of school I am extremely consistent in checking homework, examining class work, administering quizzes, giving examinations, and evaluating effort and conduct. Some students need to "find out the hard way" that "I say what I mean and I mean what I say." By the end of September I expect students to have a better understanding of classroom procedures and consequences. On the feast of the Guardian Angels (October 2) I lead the class in a prayer service. I explain that new beginnings are hard and I ask questions like, "What kinds of things how you found difficult about life in this classroom since September?" or "How many of you wish that you had been more prepared for such-and-such quiz?" or "How many of you now understand the consequences for failure to turn in an assignment?" I ask for explanations of the procedures or the cooperation-self-control policy. The questions are based on the class performance for September. I ask, "How many of you wish you had an angel who could erase those things from my mark book or from my memory?" Then I tell them that they do have a Guardian Angel and on this *one day only* their angel has convinced me to give everyone a new start. I announce that "Today is REDEMPTION DAY." I explain that I eliminated from my mark book such-and-such. I return conduct demerits and instruct the students to tear them up and throw them away. I announce that we will begin anew and because we have had a month to learn the expectations and consequences, all choices and performance will count from this day forth. There is usually great rejoicing in the classroom!

"Take a Good Look" Journaling
Cathleen Woodson (Religion Teacher, Grades 7-8, St. Vincent Ferrer School, Vallejo, CA)

Challenge students to try to make a positive connection with at least one person a day and to find a way, through words or actions, to lift up the spirit and/or influence someone else in a positive way. On the following day invite the class to write a paper on "Taking A Good Look Reflection" in which students ask themselves if they have been successful in influencing someone in a positive way. As the year progresses I see many instances of spontaneous kindness and through the writing exercise I see the children discovering new approaches to situations that they handled less positively when they were not in the practice of writing.

Two Compliments
Joan Smith (English Teacher, Grades 6-8, St. Mel School, Fair Oaks, CA)

During the course of a school day it can be easy to make a sarcastic comment or joke at the expense of another. If a student or teacher makes such a comment, no matter how innocent, the offender must give two compliments to the victim. The compliments must be specific, skill related, validating, respectful, i.e., "I admire …, I appreciate …, I enjoy …, I respect …, etc. The key is for the teacher to set up a scenario in which a brave student calls the teacher to accountability, i.e., "Mrs. Smith, I think you owe Johnny two compliments." The two compliments are given and the teaching day resumes.

Virtues, Values, and Morality Everyday
Rita Gifford (Grade 8, St. Mel School, Fair Oaks, CA)

I read aloud daily from *The One Year Book of Devotions for Kids* by Tyndale House Publishers, Inc. There is one story for each day of the year. After the story is read, students write journal responses to two or three questions. We discuss responses and then I read the given scripture passage that is pertinent to the story. These stories deal with virtues, values, and everyday morality. They teach students that to know what is right is easy; to do what is right is the hard part!

We Have a Dream
S. Carol Anne Nagel, IHM (Grades 5-8, Holy Innocents School, Philadelphia, PA)

This is an incentive to acceptable behavior or performance in the form of a student-completed bulletin board. It is most useful in January and February. Arrange a bulletin board with the words of Dr. Martin Luther King, Jr. "I Have a Dream," in patriotic colors. Attach a large white rectangular piece of cardboard or paper containing a flag outline. Hang the rectangle horizontally or vertically, depending on preference. With a pencil, create columns in the blue star "field" and draw lines to mark off the "stripes" of the flag. Create enough areas so that each student has one. At the top or bottom of column or stripe area print student initials. The flag would is a composite of student areas. *Pre-requisite*: Students have discussed appropriate target behaviors that need improvement and, with teacher approval, have chosen one or two for concentrated effort. As students work through the day, they mark a tally, at periodic intervals, showing that they "caught themselves being good" at their target behavior. Five or more tallies per day permits them to attach red, white, or blue stickers, one or two at a time, to the white bulletin board in their area." Then watch the American flag take form!

Practices Suggested by Teachers of Grades 9 - 12

Immediate Focus
Ted Venne (Grade 11 Math, Father Mercredi High School, Alberta Canada)

When students come into class at the start of the period I have an outline on the board that states the assignments that are due, quizzes or exams that are coming up, announcements that pertain to that particular class, and the lesson to be covered. The students focus on the board, what is required, and the topic to be taught. It eliminates many questions and puts more emphasis on the students and their work. A transparency and overhead projector would serve the same purpose.

Library Book Stewardship

S. M. Joanne McKelvey, IHM (Bishop Denis J. O'Connell High School, Arlington, VA)

When confronting a student who has torn pages from a library book or damaged a book in some other way, discern the most effective way to help the student: 1. to understand the seriousness of his or her actions; 2. to realize the material was not theirs to take; 3. to know the harm done to the rights of others; 4. to see the moral wrong; and 5. to make restitution and reconciliation.

Meeting them Halfway

S. Christine V. O'Donnell (Bishop Denis J. O'Connell High School, Arlington, VA)

I have had the experience where a student misbehaved or failed to complete work and because of these choices and a difficult attitude we got off to a bad start together. When I found myself becoming frustrated and irritated with the student, I realized that we needed a new start. So I asked the student to try harder while I would also try harder to be patient and supportive. Perhaps it seems like "making a deal," but it works with older students because they view you as a person and team player.

Moral Dialogue

Patricia McCormack (Grades 9-12, Archbishop Mitty High School, San Jose, CA)

Create a reflection sheet for use during a disciplinary encounter. Ask questions that focus on Reflection, Response, Restitution, and Reconciliation. 1. What values (virtues) were present or needed during the disciplinary episode? 2. How do your choices reflect the purpose or mission of our school, our tradition, our Catholic identity? 3. If you had it to do all over again, how could you achieve your goal while acting socially responsible? 4. How will you make restitution? 5. What will it take for you to experience reconciliation? How can I help that process?

NYPD BLUE (Detective Sipowitz says "Write!")
S. Rita Lenihan, IHM (St. Maria Goretti High School, Philadelphia, PA)

Following the procedures of interrogation from NYPB Blue, have yellow legal pads on hand for those times when students need to tell you their side of an incident of misbehavior. Instruct the student to write down what happened and then schedule a follow-up time to discuss the case. Having the student write out the incident or negative feelings will give all concerned time to cool off, clarify, and identify what really occurred.

Pro-Active Potpouri
Anonymous (Fort McMurray Catholic School District Schools, Alberta, Canada)

1. On Mondays have students cite weekly goals. 2. Recognize good work and effort. Create incentives, not punishment. 3. Schedule extra help sessions regularly for students. 4. Welcome questions. Create an atmosphere of openness so that students can express themselves and get assistance with decisions. 5. Be willing to listen. Seek first to understand before being understood (St. Francis of Assisi and Steve Covey) 6. Do not jump to rash decisions with respect to consequences for actions. Work with the student to help him or her understand what could have been done differently. Let the student come up with suggestions on how to deal with the situation. Use natural consequences as often as possible. 7. Forgive! Forgive! Forgive! Forgive!

Subliminal Sentences
S. Rita Lenihan, IHM (St. Maria Goretti High School, Philadelphia, PA)

Decorate the front bulletin board with a poster that proclaims, *"For success, attitude is as important as ability."* Arrange words or phrases of positive behaviors around the poster, i.e., Be Fair, Think of Others, Respect, Self-Control, Courtesy, Honesty, Think for Yourself, Cooperate, etc. Even without commenting on the bulletin board the students will pick up these attitudes. With instructional development of each trait in class, positive behavior increases. I used this idea in my Junior/Senior classroom one year and the conduct in the room was never better! Change the subliminal message and characteristics seasonally.

Conclusion

Eighty teacher practices have been shared in this chapter, eighty techniques to involve students in self-government, moral reflection, cooperative participation, respect for differences, celebration of effort, and organizational skills. The ideas are as varied as the teachers who offer them; what they have in common is their focus on providing students with experiences that are positive, purposeful, proactive, self-regulatory, instructive, and formational. It is important to realize that any idea whose goal is to form attitudes of self-discipline requires repetition. Like good habits, teacher disciplinary practices require repeated application over time in order to take root. One teacher was taught that lesson from a student. She was struggling to find a way to motivate cooperative behavior in her sixth-grade class. She tried several ideas that had worked for other teachers, she read books, and she searched the internet, but felt unsuccessful in each application. Then she sought the advice of a formation education consultant. After lengthy discussion the teacher formulated a plan and took it to her class on the following Monday morning. She explained the latest system thoroughly. Later that day the teacher was alone in the classroom with one student. She asked the student what she thought about the new plan to manage behavior and to motivate cooperation. The student said she thought the plan was fine. The teacher then asked the student if she thought the plan would work. The sixth grade student replied: *"Yes, but the other plans would have also worked if you stuck to them long enough."* It takes time and patience for ideas to take root.

What are your disciplinary practices? Do they correspond to the Gospel-driven definition of discipline? The goal is produce self-control, virtue, and discipleship. Your classroom management techniques are appropriate and life-giving to the degree that your style of leadership leads to those results. D.L. Nolte and R. Harris identified leadership and effect in the poem, *Children Learn What They Live*. If you allow each line of the poem to be matter for examination of conscience and a direction for you in the year ahead, you will be a catalyst for discipleship for your students.

> "*Children Learn What They Live:*
> *If children live with criticism, they learn to condemn.*
> *If children lie with hostility, they learn to fight.*
> *If children live with fear, they learn to be apprehensive.*
> *If children live with pity, they learn to feel sorry for themselves.*
> *If children live with ridicule, they learn to feel shy.*
> *If children live with jealousy, they learn to feel envy.*
> *If children live with shame, they learn to feel guilty.*
> *If children live with encouragement, they learn confidence.*
> *If children live with praise, they learn appreciation.*
> *If children live with acceptance, they learn to love.*
> *If children live with approval, they learn to like themselves.*
> *If children live with recognition, they learn it is good to have a goal.*
> *If children live with sharing, they learn generosity.*
> *If children live with honesty, they learn truthfulness.*
> *If children live with fairness, they learn justice.*
> *If children live with kindness and consideration, they learn respect.*
> *If children live with security, they learn to have faith in themselves and in those about them.*
> *If children live with friendliness, they learn the world is a nice place in which to live.*"[109]

Bibliography

Abidin, R. *Parenting Skills: Trainer's Manual*. Second edition. New York: Human Sciences Press, Inc, 1982.

Adler, A. *The Practice and Theory of Individual Psychology*. New York: Harcourt, 1927.

Adler, A. "The Use of Heredity and Environment," in *The Individual Psychology of Alfred Adler* (New York: Harper & Row, 1956), 205-209.

Albert, Linda and DeSisto, Pete. *Cooperative Discipline*. Circle Pines, MN: American Guidance Service, 1996.

Ansbacher, eds. *The Individual Psychology of Alfred Adler*. New York: Harper & Row, 1956, 205-209.

Archdiocese of Los Angeles. (2003, April 13). *Principles of Catholic social teaching* [weblink]. *Office of Justice and Peace*. Los Angeles, CA: Author. Retrieved April 13, 2003 from: www.ojp.la-archdiocese.org/CST6prin.htm

Benson, P. L. & Guerra, M. J. *Sharing the Faith: the Beliefs and Values of Catholic High School Teachers*. Washington, D.C.: National Catholic Educational Association, 1985.

Bettelheim, B. *A Good Enough Parent*. New York: Alfred A. Knopf, Inc., 1987.

Canter, Lee and Canter, Marlene. *Lee Canter's Assertive Discipline: Positive Behavior Management for Today's Classroom*. Santa Monica, CA: Lee Canter & Associates, 1997.

Card, M. "Could it be?" on *Present Reality* [cassette]. CA: The Sparrow Corporation, 1988.

The Catechism of the Catholic Church. Liguori, MO: Liguori Publications, 1994.

Cimino, C. "Clarifying Eternity: Providing for the Religious Experience of Students," *Momentum* 31 (September/October 2000), 18-20.

Coloroso, B. *Kids are worth it!* Revised Edition. New York: Harper Collins Publishers, Inc, 2002.

Congregation for Catholic Education. *The Catholic School on the Threshold of the Third Millennium*. Boston, MA: Pauline Books & Media, 1998.

Convey, J. *Catholic Schools Make a Difference*. Washington, D.C.: National Catholic Educational Association, 1992.

Cook, T.J. *Architects of Catholic Culture: Designing and Building Catholic Culture in Catholic Schools*. Washington, D.C.: National Catholic Educational Association, 2001.

Coombe, D.M. "Catholic Social Teaching." *Momentum* 30 (August/September 1999), 60.

Coopersmith, S. *The Antecedents of Self Esteem*. San Francisco: Freeman, 1967.

Curwin, R. L. & Mendler, A. N. *Discipline with Dignity*. Alexandria, VA: Association for Supervision and Curriculum Development, 1999.

DeBruyn, R. L. & Larson, J.L. *You Can Handle Them All*. Manhattan, Kansas: The MASTER Teacher, Inc, 1984.

Dinkmeyer, D. & Dinkmeyer, D., Jr. "Adlerian approaches," in H. T. Prout & D. T. Brown, eds. *Counseling and Psychotherapy with Children and Adolescents: Theory and Practice for School and Clinic Settings* (Brandon: Clinical Psychology Publishing Co., Inc., 1983), 289-327.

Dinkmeyer, D. & McKay, G. *Parenting Teenagers*. Second Edition. Circle Pines, MN: American Guidance Service, 1990.

Dinkmeyer, D. & McKay, G. *The Parent's Handbook: Systematic Training for Effective Parenting*. Third Edition. Circle Pines, MN: American Guidance Service, 1989.

Dinkmeyer, D., & McKay, G. *Raising a Responsible Child*. New York: Simon & Schuster, 1996.

Dinkmeyer, D., McKay, G., Dinkmeyer, J., Dinkmeyer, D., Jr., and McKay, J., Jr. *Parenting Young Children*. Circle Pines, MN: American Guidance Service, 1997.

Dreikurs, R. *The Challenge of Parenthood*. Second Edition. New York: Penguin Books USA Inc., 1958.

Dreikurs, R. *Children: the Challenge*. Second Edition. New York: Penguin Books USA Inc., 1964.

Dreikurs, R., & Soltz, V. *Children: The Challenge*. New York: Hawthorn Books, 1964.

Erikson, E. *Childhood and Society*. Third Edition. New York: Norton, 1985.

Freiberg, H. Jerome. *CMCD/Consistency, Management and Cooperative Discipline*. www.cmcd.coe.uh.edu, 2002.

Ginott, H.G. *Teacher and Child: A Book for Parents and Teachers*. New York: The Macmillan Company, 1972.

Green, S. "Find Us Faithful," on *Find Us Faithful* [compact disk]. Chatsworth, CA: The Sparrow Corporation, 1988.

Groome, T. "What Makes a School Catholic?" in T. McLaughlin, J. O'Keefe, & B. O'Keefe, eds. *The Contemporary Catholic School: Context, Identity and Diversity*. (Washington, D.C.: Falmer Press, 1996), 107-125.

Hudson, W. *Discipline and Discipleship: The Role of Catholic Identity in Shaping Disciplinary Procedures* (Cassette Recording No. 01012-3229). Washington, D.C.: National Catholic Educational Association. Presentation at the 97th Annual Convention, Baltimore, MD, April, 2000; and at the 98th Annual Convention, Milwaukee, WI, April, 2001.

Hudson, W. *Discipline or Discipleship: the Role of Catholic Identity in Shaping a School's Disciplinary Procedures.* University of St. Thomas, Research Proposal, June, 1998.

John Paul II. *Familiaris Consortio (On the Family).* Washington, D.C.: United States Catholic Conference, 1981.

John Paul II. *The Members of Christ's Faithful People.* Boston: Daughters of St. Paul, 1988.

John Paul II. *Mission of the Redeemer.* Boston: St. Paul Books & Media. 1990.

John Paul II. *Novo Millennio Ineunte (At the Beginning of the New Millennium).* Boston, MA: Pauline Books & Media, 2000.

Kealey, R. J. "St. John Baptist de La Salle: Principal Patron Before God of All Teachers of Youth," *Momentum* 31(September/October 2000), 12-14.

Kohn, A. *Beyond Discipline: From Compliance to Community.* Alexandria, VA: Association for Supervision and Curriculum Development, 1996.

Lonergan, Bernard. *Method in Theology.* Second Edition. New York: Herder and Herder, 1973.

Malone, J. "Listening with the Heart," *Human Development* 21 (2000), 13-17.

Marshall, M. *Discipline Without Stress, Punishments or Rewards.* Los Alamitos, CA: Piper Press, 2001.

Master Teacher. *You Can Handle Them All* [Video Series]. (Available from The MASTER Teacher, Inc., P.O. Box 1207, Manhattan, Kansas 66506), 1991.

Master Teacher. *Discipline Techniques You Can Master in a Minute* [Video Series]. (Available from The MASTER Teacher, Inc., P.O. Box 1207, Manhattan, Kansas 66506), 1995.

Master Teacher. *Great Classroom Management* [Video Series]. (Available from The MASTER Teacher, Inc., P.O. Box 1207, Manhattan, Kansas 66506), 2002.

McCarty, M. *Deciding.* Orlando: Brown-Roa, Harcourt Brace & Company, 1999.

McCormack, P.M. *Catholic Elementary Schools as Agents of Parent Formation Needs as Perceived by Parents* (Doctoral dissertation, University of San Francisco). *Dissertation Abstracts International, 56* (02), p. 420. (UMI No. 9526343), 1995.

McCormack, P. M. "Family Essentials for Positive Soul Formation," *Today's Catholic Teacher* 35 (August/September 2001), 22-32.

McCormack, P. M. "Fostering Discipline: Discerning Voices for Life-Giving Choices," *Today's Catholic Teacher* 33 (August/September 1999), 46-49.

McCormack, P. M. *Fostering Student Self-Esteem in the Catholic Elementary School*. Washington, D.C.: National Catholic Educational Association, 1999.

McCormack, P. M. "A Parent's Guide to Fostering Self Discipline: The Connection Between Needs and Behavior," *Today's Catholic Teacher* 33 (November/December 1999), 46-47.

McCormack, P. M. "A Parent's Guide to Fostering Self Discipline: Consequences vs. Punishments and Rewards," *Today's Catholic Teacher* 33 (March 2000), 56-57.

McCormack, P. M. "A Parent's Guide to Fostering Self Discipline: Encouragement Versus Praise," *Today's Catholic Teacher* 33 (April 2000), 74-75.

McCormack, P. M. "A Parent's Guide to Fostering Self Discipline: Parent Authority Style," *Today's Catholic Teacher* 33 (October 1999), 54-55.

McCormack, P. M. "A Parent's Guide for Soul Formation: Communicating Genuine Affection," *Today's Catholic Teacher* 35 (March 2002), 64-65.

McCormack, P.M. "A Parent's Guide for Soul Formation: Developing Competence, Establishing Industry," *Today's Catholic Teacher* 35 (January/February 2002), 56-57.

McCormack, P. M. "A Parent's Guide for Soul Formation: Igniting Hope, Establishing Security," *Today's Catholic Teacher* 35 (August/September 2001), 34-35.

McCormack, P. M. "A Parent's Guide for Soul Formation: Instilling Purpose, Establishing Initiative," *Today's Catholic Teacher* 35 (November/December 2001), 38-39.

McCormack, P. M. "A Parent's Guide for Soul Formation: Strengthening Willpower, Establishing Autonomy," *Today's Catholic Teacher* 35 (October 2001), 34-35.

McDonald, M. "Missionaries of the New Millennium," *Momentum* 31 (September/October 2000), 23-24.

McNamee, P. "A Principal's Joy," *Momentum* 31 (September/October 2000), 25-26.

National Conference of Catholic Bishops. *To Teach as Jesus Did*. Washington, D.C.: National Conference of Catholic Bishops, 1972.

Nelsen, J. *Positive Discipline*. New York: Ballantine Books, 1987.

Nelsen, J., Lott, L., & Glenn, S. *Positive Discipline in the Classroom*. Third Revised Edition. Roseville, CA: Prima Publishing, 2000.

Nelsen, J., Duffy, R., Escobar, L., Ortolano, K., & Owen-Sohocki, D. *Positive Discipline: A Teacher's A-Z Guide*. Second Revised Edition. Roseville, CA: Prima Publishing, 2001.

Nolte, D. L. & Harris, R. *Children Learn What They Live: Parenting to Inspire Values*. New York: Workman Publishing, 1998.

Paul VI, Pope. *The Pope Speaks*, Vol. 11. Washington, D.C.: TPS Publications, 1966.

Paul VI, Pope. *The Teachings of Pope Paul VI: 1975*. Vatican City: Libreria Editrice Vaticana, 1998.

Popkin, M. H. *Active Parenting Today*. Atlanta, Georgia: Active Parenting Publishers, 1993.

Prochaska, L.M. *Living a Moral Life*. Mission Hills, CA: Benziger Publishing Co., 1992.

Roach, A.D. "The Passion of My Life," *Momentum* 31 (September / October 2000), 22.

The Sacramentary of the Roman Missal. New York: Catholic Book Publishing Company, 1985.

Sergiovanni, T. J. *Building Community in Schools*. San Francisco: Jossey-Bass, 1994.

Troccoli, K. "May I Be His Love," On *Sounds of Heaven* [CD]. Reunion Records, 1995.

United States Catholic Conference. *Teach Them*. Washington, D.C.: United States Catholic Conference, 1976.

United States Catholic Conference. *Sharing Catholic Social Teaching: Challenges and Directions*. Washington, D.C.: United States Catholic Conference, 1998.

United States Catholic Conference. Congregation for Catholic Education. *The Catholic School*. Washington, D.C.: United States Catholic Conference, 1977.

United States Catholic Conference. Congregation for Catholic Education. *Lay Catholics in Schools: Witnesses to the Faith*. Boston: Daughters of St. Paul, 1982.

United States Catholic Conference. Congregation for Catholic Education. *The Religious Dimension of Education in a Catholic School*. Washington, D.C.: United States Catholic Conference, 1988.

Vatican Council II. *Declaration on Christian Education*. In W.Z.M. Abbott (ed.), *The Documents of Vatican II*. New York: Herder & Herder, 1965.

Wadell, P. J. *Morality: A Course on Catholic Living*. New York: William H. Sadlier, Inc, 1998.

Watson, G. *Classroom Discipline Problem Solver*. Indianapolis, IN: Jossey-Bass, 1998.

Wong, H. K. & Wong, R. T. *The First Days of School*. Sunnyvale, CA: Harry K. Wong Publications, Inc, 1998.

Wong, H. K. *The Effective Teacher* [Video Series]. (Available from Harry K. Wong Publications, Inc., 943 North Shoreline Boulevard, Mountain View, CA 94043), 1996.

Yancey, P. *What's So Amazing About Grace*. Grand Rapids: Zondervan, 1997.

Endnotes

¹ The proto-Latin verb *discipere* means to analyze intellectually or thoroughly. It comes from *dis+capere* (to take apart).

² The verse, by C.A. Hall, can be found in *Hoyt's New Cyclopedia of Practical Quotations* (New York: Funk & Wagnalls, 1922), 346.

³ P.M. McCormack, "Fostering Discipline: Discerning Voices for Life-Giving Choices," *Today's Catholic Teacher* 33 (1999), 46.

⁴ Cf. *The Catechism of the Catholic Church* (Liguori, MO: Liguori Publications, 1994), nos. 1255, 1653, and 1656.

⁵ Vatican II. *Declaration on Christian Education* (1965), in W.Z.M. Abbot (ed.), *The Documents of Vatican II* (New York: Herder & Herder, 1965); United States Catholic Conference. Congregation for Catholic Education, *The Catholic School*. Washington, D.C.: United States Catholic Conference, 1977, hereafter cited as *The Catholic School*; United States Catholic Conference. Congregation for Catholic Education, *Lay Catholics in Schools: Witnesses to the Faith*. Washington, D.C. United States Catholic Conference, 1982; United States Catholic Conference. Congregation for Catholic Education, *The Religious Dimension of Education in a Catholic School*. Washington, D.C.: United States Catholic Conference, 1988, hereafter cited as *The Religious Dimension*; John Paul II, *Familiaris Consortio (On the Family)*. Washington, D.C. United States Catholic Conference, 1981; John Paul II, *The Members of Christ's Faithful People*. Boston: Daughters of St. Paul, 1988; National Conference of Catholic Bishops, *To Teach as Jesus Did*. Washington, D.C.: National Conference of Catholic Bishops, 1972; and United States Catholic Conference, *Teach Them*. Washington, D.C.: United States Catholic Conference, 1976.

⁶ *The Religious Dimension*," #43.

⁷ P.M. McCormack, *Catholic Elementary Schools as Agents of Parent Formation Needs as Perceived by Parents* (Doctoral Dissertation, University of San Francisco, 1995), 41. Available through Dissertation Abstracts International 56, 420 (UMI No. 9526343), hereafter cited as *Catholic Elementary Schools*.

⁸ *The Catholic School*, #45.

9   *Catholic Elementary Schools,* 36-37.

10   Ibid.

11   *Religious Dimension,* #82-89.

12   Ibid., #9.

13   *The Catholic School,* #45.

14   *The Catholic School on the Threshold,* #4.

15   Ibid., #6.

16   *Note:* Throughout this book the terms *teacher* or *educator* are used to indicate all adults who form the teaching community within the Catholic school, i.e., administrators, classroom teachers, resource specialists, auxiliary personnel, salaried staff persons, etc.

17   Lee Canter and Marlene Canter, *Lee Canter's Assertive Discipline: Positive Behavior Management for Today's Classroom* (Santa Monica, CA: Lee Canter & Assoc., 1997); Linda Albert and Pete DeSisto, *Cooperative Discipline* (Circle Pines, MN: American Guidance Service, Inc., 1996); H. Jerome Freiberg, *CMCD/Consistency Management and Cooperative Discipline* (www.cmcd.coe.uh.edu, 2002); Marvin Marshall, *Discipline without Stress, Punishments or Rewards* (Los Alamitos, CA: Piper Press, 2001).

18   Lickona, as cited by William J. Hudson, "Discipline and Discipleship: The Role of Catholic Identity in Shaping a School's Disciplinary Procedures," (Research Proposal, University of St. Thomas. 1998), 5; and William J. Hudson, "Discipline and Discipleship: The Role of Catholic Identity in Shaping Disciplinary Procedures." Washington, D.C.: National Catholic Educational Association. Presentation at the 97th Annual Convention, Baltimore, MD, April, 2000; and at the 98th Annual Convention, Milwaukee, WI, April, 2001 (Cassette Recording No. 01012-3229).

19   *The Catholic School on the Threshold,* #14.

20   Hudson, op cit.; and A. Kohn. *Beyond Discipline: From Compliance to Community* (Alexandria, VA: Association for Supervision and Curriculum Development, 1996).

21   Hudson, op cit.

22   Ibid., "Discipline and Discipleship," 4-5, citing Marshall, 1998, and presentation.

23   B. Lonergan, *Method in Theology.* 2nd ed. (New York: Herder and Herder, 1973), 130-131.

24   Ibid., 240.

25   Hudson, "Discipline or Discipleship" Presentation at NCEA annual meetings, 2000, 2001.

26   B. Coloroso. *Kids Are Worth It!* Rev. ed. (New York: Harper Collins Publishers, Inc., 2002), 79.

27 Kohn, 101-102. See also, T.J. Sergiovanni. *Building Community in Schools* (San Francisco: Jossey-Bass, 1994).

28 Hudson, "Discipline or Discipleship," presentations at NCEA annual meetings, 2000, 2001.

29 James Baldwin, weblink: www.famous-quotations.com

30 R. Newman, *African American Quotations* (Phoenix: The Oryx Press, 1998), 278.

31 See Augustine's *Confessions,* available in many editions.

32 Marshall, *Discipline Without Stress, Punishments, or Rewards: How Teachers and Parents Promote Responsibility and Learning* (Los Alamitos, CA: Piper Press, 2001).

33 Personal Communication, March 18, 2003.

34 Personal Communication, March 4, 2003.

35 T.J. Cook, *Architects of Catholic Culture: Designing and Building Catholic Culture in Catholic Schools* (Washington, D.C.: National Catholic Educational Association, 2001), 23.

36 United States Catholic Conference, *Sharing Catholic Social Teaching: Challenges and Directions* (Washington, D.C.: United States Catholic Conference, 1998), 4, 23.

37 Cook, 22.

38 Cf. Hudson; see also D.M. Coombe, "Catholic Social Teaching," *Momentum* 30 (August/September 1999), 60. See also the Archdiocese of Los Angeles. Office of Justice and Peace, *Principles of Catholic Social Teaching* (www.ojp.la-archdiocese.org/CST6prin.htm).

39 M. McCarty. *Deciding* (Orlando: Brown-ROA, Harcourt Brace & Company, 1999), 197.

40 *The Sacramentary of the Roman Missal* (New York: Catholic Book Publishing Company, 1985), 557.

41 Pope Paul VI. *The Pope Speaks,* Vol. 11 (Washington, D.C.: TPS Publications, 1966), 365.

42 *The Sacramentary of the Roman Missal,* 556-567.

43 P.J. Wadell. *Morality: A Course on Catholic Living* (New York: William H. Sadlier, Inc., 1998), 119.

44 Pope Paul VI, *The Teachings of Pope Paul VI: 1975,* Vol. 8 (Vatican City: Libreria Editrice Vaticana, 1975), 60.

45 L.M. Prochaska, *Living a Moral Life* (Mission Hills, CA: Benziger Publishing Co., 1992), 86-87.

46 Coloroso, 88.

47 *The Teachings of Pope Paul VI: 1975,* 64.

48 Kohn, 115.

49 McCarty, 279.

50 *The Teachings of Pope Paul VI: 1975,* 162.

51 *The Catholic School on the Threshold,* #19.

52 Kohn, 111.

53 Hudson, Presentations at NCEA annual meetings, 2000, 2001.

54 Hudson, op cit.

55 John Paul II, *Novo Millennio Ineunte: At the Beginning of the New Millennium* (Boston: Pauline Books and Media, 2000), #43.

56 John Paul II, *Mission of the Redeemer* (Boston: St. Paul Books & Media, 1990), #11.

57 *Ibid.*, #20.

58 Robert J. Kealey, "St. John Baptist de La Salle: Principal Patron Before God of All Teachers of Youth," *Momentum* 31 (September/October 2000), 14.

59 Carol Cimino, "Clarifying Eternity: Providing for the Religious Experience of Students," *Momentum* 31 (September/October 2000), 20.

60 A.D. Roach, "The Passion of My Life," *Momentum* 31 (September/October 2000), 22.

61 Mary MacDonald, "Missionaries of the New Millennium," *Momentum* 31 (September/October 2000), 24.

62 Patricia McNamee, "A Principal's Joy," *Momentum* 31 (September/October 2000), 26.

63 Frederick Buechner. Prayer given at a Philips Exeter Academy commencement between 1958-1967. Personal Communication, July 1, 2003.

64 *The Catholic School,* #43.

65 John Convey, *Catholic Schools Make a Difference* (Washington, D.C.: National Catholic Educational Association, 1992), 111-112.

66 *The Catholic School on the Threshold,* #18.

67 Convey, 112.

68 R.W. Emerson, *Letters and Social Aims* (Boston: Houghton, Mifflin and Company, 1894), 95.

69 To see this quotation, go to: www.quotablequotes.net.

70 *The Catholic School on the Threshold,* #15.

71 H.G. Ginott. *Teacher and Child: A Book for Parents and Teachers* (New York: The Macmillan Company, 1972), 149-150.

72 S. Green, *Find Us Faithful* (compact disk). Chatsworth, CA: The Sparrow Corporation, 1988.

73 R. Abidin, *Parenting Skills: Trainer's Manual,* Second Edition. New York: Human Sciences Press, Inc., 1982; A. Adler, *The Practice and Theory of Individual Psychology* (New York: Harcourt, 1927) and "The Use of Heredity and Environment," in *The Individual Psychology of Alfred Adler* (New York: Harper & Row, 1956), 205-209; S. Coopersmith, *The Antecedents of Self Esteem* (San Francisco: Freeman, 1967); D. Dinkmeyer and D. Dinkmeyer, Jr., "Adlerian Approaches," in H.T.

Prout & D. T. Brown (eds.). *Counseling and Psychotherapy With Children and Adolescents: Theory and Practice for School and Clinic Settings* (Brandon: Clinical Psychology Publishing Co., Inc., 1983), 289-327; D. Dinkmeyer & G. McKay, *The Parent's Handbook: Systematic Training for Effective Parenting*, Third edition (Circle Pines, MN: American Guidance Service, 1989); R. Dreikurs, *The Challenge of Parenthood*, Second edition (New York: Penguin Books, 1958); and, E. Erikson, *Childhood and Society*, Third edition (New York: Norton, 1985).

[74] J. Malone. "Listening with the Heart," *Human Development* 21 (2000), 13-17.

[75] Ginott, 150.

[76] Dinkmeyer & McKay, op cit.; Dreikurs, op cit; J. Nelsen. *Positive Discipline* (New York: Ballantine Books, 1987); M.H. Popkin, *Active Parenting Today*. Atlanta: Active Parenting Publishers, 1993.

[77] P.M. McCormack, "A Parent's Guide to Fostering Self Discipline: Parent Authority Style," *Today's Catholic Teacher* 33 (1999), 54.

[78] Ibid., 55.

[79] Ginott, 15.

[80] Cf. Dinkmeyer & McKay, Dreikurs, Nelsen, Popkin, op cit.

[81] D. Dinkmeyer & G. McKay, *Parenting Teenagers*, Second edition (Circle Pines, MN: American Guidance Service, 1990), p. 10-14.

[82] P.M. McCormack, "A Parent's Guide to Fostering Self Discipline: The Connection Between Needs and Behavior," *Today's Catholic Teacher* 33 (1999), 46-47.

[83] STEP Literature: D. Dinkmeyer, G. McKay, J. Dinkmeyer, D. Dinkmeyer, Jr., J.McKay, *Parenting Young Children*, (Circle Pines, MN: American Guidance Service, 1997); D. Dinkmeyer and G. McKay. *The Parent's Handbook*, op cit.; *Parenting Teenagers*, op cit.

[84] R.L. DeBruyn and J.L. Larson, *You Can Handle Them All* (Manhattan, KS: The MASTER Teacher, Inc., 1984).

[85] See P.M. McCormack, *Fostering Student Self-Esteem in the Catholic Elementary School* (Washington, D.C.: National Catholic Educational Association, 1999), for detailed information. Cited hereafter as *Fostering Student Self-Esteem*.

[86] P.M. McCormack, "Family Essentials for Positive Soul Formation," *Today's Catholic Teacher* 35 (August/September 2001), 22-32.

[87] P.M. McCormack, "A Parent's Guide for Soul Formation: Igniting Hope, Establishing Security," *Today's Catholic Teacher* 35 (August/September 2001), 34.

[88] *Fostering Student Self-Esteem*, 10-22, for ideas that foster security development in classrooms.

[89] P.M. McCormack, "A Parent's Guide for Soul Formation: Strengthening Willpower, Establishing Autonomy," *Today's Catholic Teacher* 35 (October 2001), 34.

90   *Fostering Student Self-Esteem.* See, especially, 27-38, for timely, practical ideas that foster autonomy development in the classroom.

91   P.M. McCormack, "A Parent's Guide For Soul Formation: Instilling Purpose, Establishing Initiative," *Today's Catholic Teacher* 35 (November/December 2001), 38.

92   See *Fostering Student Self-Esteem,* 43-52, for additional examples suggested by a body of teachers.

93   P.M. McCormack, "A Parent's Guide for Soul Formation: Developing Competence, Establishing Industry," *Today's Catholic Teacher* 35 (2002), 56-57.

94   *"Fostering Student Self-Esteem,* 57-63.

95   P. Yancey, *What's So Amazing About Grace* (Grand Rapids, Michigan: Zondervan, 1997), 70.

96   P.M. McCormack, "A Parent's Guide for Soul Formation: Communicating Genuine Affection," *Today's Catholic Teacher* 35 (March 2002), 64-65.

97   Nelsen, *Positive Discipline,* 205.

98   D. Dinkmeyer and G. McKay. *Raising a Responsible Child* (New York: Simon & Schuster, 1996), 48.

99   See *Fostering Student Self-Esteem,* 65-66. See 66-71, for a complete list of subcategories.

100 It would be well worth the time of the reader to think about the specific advice of these students which is found on pages 72-76 of *Fostering Student Self Esteem.*

101 P.M. McCormack, "A Parent's Guide to Fostering Self-Discipline: Consequences vs. Punishments and Rewards," *Today's Catholic Teacher* 33 (March 2000), 56.

102 Coloroso, 50.

103 B. Bettelheim, *A Good Enough Parent* (New York: Alfred A. Knopf, Inc., 1987), 166.

104 Dinkmeyer & McKay, *The Parent's Handbook,* 78-82.

105 R.L. Curwin and A.N. Mendler. *Discipline With Dignity* (Alexandria, VA: Association for Supervision and Curriculum Development, 1999), 71.

106 P.M. McCormack, "A Parent's Guide to Fostering Self-Discipline: Encouragement versus Praise," *Today's Catholic Teacher* 33 (April 2000), 74.

107 Sister Carol Nagel, IHM, personal communication, July 12, 2002.

108 H.K. Wong. *The Effective Teacher* [Video Series, 1996]. Available from Harry K. Wong Publications, Inc., 943 North Shoreline Boulevard, Mountain View, CA 94043.

109 D.L. Nolte and R. Harris. *Children Learn What They Live: Parenting to Inspire Values* (Workman Publishing, 1998), vi, vii.

About the Author

PATRICIA M. MCCORMACK, Ed. D., is a formation education consultant whose ministry focuses on the spiritual, psychological, and social development of children. Her history in Catholic education includes elementary and secondary teaching, elementary school principalship, college instructor, teacher education preparation, and adjunct teaching at Immaculata University, Spalding University, and the Catholic University of America, where she is an associate of the Center for the Advancement of Catholic Education. She holds a bachelor's degree in Theology and Sociology from Immaculata University, a master's degree in K-8 education from Rowan University, and a doctorate in private school administration from the Institute for Catholic Educational Leadership, University of San Francisco. A regular speaker at NCEA conventions, Dr. McCormack has presented numerous workshops and lectures, both nationally and internationally. She speaks to educators and parents on formative issues, such as soulful formation, identity development, Christian character and conscience formation, self-discipline and spirituality, as well as family life. Since 1996, Dr. McCormack has provided parent education on those topics through the Parent Partnership Handbook series of *Today's Catholic Teacher* magazine. Dr. McCormack also facilitates retreat experiences for catechists, school staffs, and administrators. Currently, she is director of the Office of Formative Parenting Support Services, Newark, DE. She is the author of the 1999 NCEA text, *Fostering Student Self-Esteem in the Catholic Elementary School*. She is also the author of *Mary's Beads of Transformation*, published in 2003 by Liguori Publications.